Ninja Air Fryer
Cookbook with Pictures

Simple & Delicious Ninja Foodi Air Fryer Recipes and 4 Weeks Diet Plan for Beginners and Advanced Users

Helen Bently

TABLE OF CONTENTS

Introduction 5
- What is Ninja Foodi Air Fryer? 5
- Main Functions of Ninja Foodi Air Fryer........6
- Buttons and Users' Guide of Ninja Foodi Air Fryer 6
- Cleaning & Maintaining Tips 7

Breakfast Recipes 8
- Sausage with Eggs 8
- Breakfast Bacon 9
- Pepper Egg Cups 9
- Crispy Hash Browns 10
- Pumpkin Muffins 11
- Cinnamon Toasts 12
- Morning Egg Rolls..................................13
- Morning Patties 14
- Biscuit Balls 15
- Breakfast Sausage Omelet.....................16
- Banana and Raisins Muffins 17
- Egg with Baby Spinach...........................18
- Yellow Potatoes with Eggs 19

Snacks and Appetizers Recipes 20
- Onion Rings...20
- Crispy Tortilla Chips...............................21
- Parmesan French Fries 21
- Stuffed Bell Peppers 22
- Fried Halloumi Cheese 22
- Sweet Bites 23
- Peppered Asparagus 23
- Cheddar Quiche 24
- Crispy Plantain Chips 24
- Grill Cheese Sandwich 25
- Chicken Crescent Wraps 25
- Blueberries Muffins 26
- Chicken Tenders....................................27

Beef, Lamb and Pork Recipes 28
- Zucchini Pork Skewers 28
- Beef Cheeseburgers...............................29
- Gochujang Brisket 30
- Chipotle Beef 31
- Mustard Rubbed Lamb Chops 32
- Lamb Shank with Mushroom Sauce 33
- Ham Burger Patties................................34
- Bell Peppers with Sausages....................35
- Parmesan Pork Chops 35
- Short Ribs & Root Vegetables.................36
- Chinese BBQ Pork..................................37
- Pork Chops 37
- Steak and Mashed Creamy Potatoes..........38
- Steak in Air Fry 39
- Beef Ribs I 39
- Beef Ribs II 40

Chicken and Poultry Recipes 41
- Crusted Chicken Breast 41
- Balsamic Duck Breast............................42
- Chicken Wings 42
- Pickled Chicken Fillets 43
- Chili Chicken Wings 44
- Air Fried Turkey Breast..........................45
- Cheddar-Stuffed Chicken 45
- Brazilian Chicken Drumsticks..................46

Veggie Stuffed Chicken Breasts 47
Sweet and Spicy Carrots with Chicken Thighs
.... 48
Chicken Leg Piece 49
Yummy Chicken Breasts 49
Spiced Chicken and Vegetables 50
Chicken Breast Strips 51
Cornish Hen with Asparagus 52

Seafood and Fish Recipes 53

Salmon Patties 53
Salmon Nuggets 54
Breaded Scallops 54
Fried Lobster Tails 55
Scallops with Greens 55
Salmon with Fennel Salad 56
Two-Way Salmon 56
Seafood Shrimp Omelet 57
Salmon with Green Beans 58
Fish and Chips 59
Frozen Breaded Fish Fillet 59
Keto Baked Salmon with Pesto 60
Crusted Tilapia 60
Codfish with Herb Vinaigrette 61
Lemon Pepper Salmon with Asparagus 62

Vegetables Recipes 63

Garlic Potato Wedges in Air Fryer 63
Curly Fries 64
Fried Olives 64
Quinoa Patties 65
Sweet Potatoes with Honey Butter 66
Fried Artichoke Hearts 66

Zucchini Cakes 67
Green Beans with Baked Potatoes 67
Zucchini with Stuffing 68
Mixed Air Fry Veggies 69
Air Fried Okra 69
Fresh Mix Veggies in Air Fryer 70
Kale and Spinach Chips 70
Brussels Sprouts 71

Desserts Recipes 72

Apple Hand Pies 72
Air Fried Beignets 73
Oreo Rolls 74
Zesty Cranberry Scones 75
Walnuts Fritters 76
Biscuit Doughnuts 77
Bread Pudding 77
Pumpkin Muffins 78
Lemony Sweet Twists 79
Chocolate Chip Muffins 80
Mini Blueberry Pies 81
Air Fried Bananas 81
Mini Strawberry and Cream Pies 82

4 Weeks Diet Plan 83

Week 1 83
Week 2 84
Week 3 85
Week 4 86

Conclusion 87

Introduction

Get over the hassle of switching between different appliances to prepare your favorite meal or snack with the efficient Ninja Foodi Air Fryer. Get more space on the kitchen counter and add versatility to your cooking. It considerably cuts down your cooking time with the convenience of 4 cooking features packed into one appliance. The Ninja Foodi Air Fryer is worthy of being your perfect kitchen companion.

What is Ninja Foodi Air Fryer?

Ninja Foodi Air Fryer is a kitchen appliance that takes your cooking up a notch with multiple functions. It offers the most convenient cooking experience with its one-touch control panel providing you full control. Along with sparing space on your kitchen counter, it provides a fast and easy way to cook your meals and snacks. Using the Ninja Foodi Air Fryer, you will get 75% less fat than traditional frying methods. The 4-in-one efficient air fryer is capable of giving you golden crispy texture finish without fat and oil. So now enjoy your favorite snacks without guilt. Using and cleaning the air fryer is super easy and opens up countless cooking avenues with added functionalities.

Main Functions of Ninja Foodi Air Fryer

The powerful and efficient Ninja Foodi Air Fryer saves your cooking time and serves you healthy and delicious meals. It provides you with 4 main cooking functions; let's get to know them better.

Air Fry

You can enjoy your favorite snacks without being guilty, as the Ninja Foodi Air Fryer can prepare meals with little to no oil.

Roast

The air fryer can serve as an oven and fulfill all your roasting requests. Make your favorite roasted veggies, casseroles, and much more.

Dehydrate

The air fryer's multi-layer rack provides you with more dehydrating capacity than an average fryer. It features a combination of low fan speed and low temperature that enables thorough dehydration and gives you healthy snacks.

Reheat

You just have to press the reheat button, and the air fryer will select the default temperature to reheat and revive the leftovers gently.

Buttons and Users' Guide of Ninja Foodi Air Fryer

The Ninja Foodi Air Fryer has a straightforward control panel with buttons to operate and activate its cooking modes.

Function Buttons

The following buttons allow you to use the functions offered by the air fryer.

Air Fry: Using this function button, you can air fry your food to give it a crispy and crunchy finish with little or no oil.

Roast: The roast button lets you use the appliance as a roaster oven. You can use it for roasting tender meats, baked treats, and more.

Dehydrate: Activate the dehydrate function and prepare healthy snacks by dehydrating meats, fruits, and vegetables.

Reheat: Use the reheat button to warm the leftovers and have an evenly reheated and crisp meal.

Operating Buttons

Temp arrows: The unit has up and down temp buttons to adjust the cooking temperature. You can set the temperature before or alter it during cooking.

Time arrows: The up and down time buttons help you set the timing in all the functions.

Start/Pause button: After selecting the setting time and the desired temperature, press the Start/Pause button to initiate cooking. The button also allows you to stop cooking at any time.

Power button: As the name suggests, the power button turns the unit on or cuts off the power, shuts down the unit, and turns off all the functions.

Users' Guide

- Remove all the packaging material, labels, or tapings from the unit before the first use.
- Plug the cord into the wall outlet and then press the power button to turn it on.
- Press the button to select the function you wish to use.

- After choosing the function, you can use the time and temp buttons to select the cooking time and temperature.
- When you are done cooking, press the power button to turn it off, let it sit idle to cool down, and then clean it thoroughly.

Cleaning & Maintaining Tips

No matter how powerful an appliance is, it will lose its functionality over time if not appropriately maintained. Cleaning the unit after every use is the best way to avoid it. Here's how to clean and take good care of your Ninja Foodi Air Fryer.

Regular Cleaning

- Firstly, unplug the unit from the power outlet before cleaning.
- Use a soft, damp cloth to clean the unit's exterior and control panel. Do not use harsh brushes or cleaners; it might damage the product.
- You can wash accessories like the crisper plate, basket, or multi-level rack in the dishwasher. The main unit is not dishwasher-safe.
- Let the basket or crisper plate soak in warm, soapy water and clean all the food residues stuck on them.
- Towel-dry or air-dry all the parts thoroughly after use. Use a soft cloth and avoid any abrasive chemicals.
- You can use a cleaning brush to remove food residues and clean the heating element.

Maintenance Tips

Regular cleaning is an absolute necessity to maintain the productivity of the unit. Apart from that, here are some points that will help you maintain the unit and extend its life and usability on your kitchen counter.

- Never wash the appliance in a dishwasher or immerse it in water. However, the accessories are dishwasher-safe.
- It's best to avoid using abrasive chemicals and harsh cleaners.
- Take the food out as soon as it's prepared to prevent overcooking.
- Do not use the appliance for deep-frying in oil.
- After cooking, let the unit cool for about 30 minutes before cleaning or storing.

Breakfast Recipes

Sausage with Eggs

Prep time: 10 minutes | **Cook time:** 12 minutes | **Serves:** 2

Ingredients

- 4 sausage links, raw and uncooked
- 4 eggs, uncooked
- 1 tablespoon green onion
- 2 tablespoons chopped tomatoes
- Salt and black pepper, to taste
- 2 tablespoons milk, dairy
- Oil spray, for greasing

Directions

1. Take a bowl and whisk eggs in it.
2. Then pour milk, and add onions and tomatoes.
3. Whisk it all well.
4. Now season it with salt and black pepper.
5. Take one cake pan, that fit inside the air fryer and grease it with oil spray.
6. Pour the omelet in the greased cake pans.
7. Slice the sausages in round shapes and top it on eggs.
8. Preheat the unit by selecting AIR FRY mode for 3 minutes at 325 degrees F.
9. Select START/PAUSE to begin the preheating process.
10. Once preheating is done, put the cake pan inside the unit.
11. Select Air Fry function of Ninja Air Fryer, and set the timer to 12 minutes at 310 degrees F.
12. Once the cooking cycle completes, serve by transferring it to plates.
13. Enjoy hot as a delicious breakfast.

Serving Suggestion: Serve it with toasted bread slices.

Variation Tip: Use almond milk if like non-dairy milk.

Nutritional Information Per Serving:

Calories 240 | Fat 18.4g | Sodium 396mg | Carbs 2.8g | Fiber0.2g | Sugar 2g | Protein 15.6g

Breakfast Bacon

Prep time: 10 minutes | **Cook time:** 14 minutes | **Serves:** 4

Ingredients:

- ½ lb. bacon slices

Preparation:

1. At 390 degrees F, preheat your Air Fryer on Air Fry mode.
2. Spread the bacon slices in the Air Fryer Basket evenly in a single layer.
3. Return the Air Fryer Basket to the Air Fryer and cook for 14 minutes.
4. Initiate cooking by pressing the START/PAUSE BUTTON.
5. Flip the crispy bacon once cooked halfway through, then resume cooking.
6. Serve.

Serving Suggestion: Serve the bacon with eggs and bread slices.

Variation Tip: Add salt and black pepper for seasoning.

Nutritional Information Per Serving:

Calories 273 | Fat 22g | Sodium 517mg | Carbs 3.3g | Fiber 0.2g | Sugar 1.4g | Protein 16.1g

Pepper Egg Cups

Prep time: 15 minutes | **Cook time:** 18 minutes | **Serves:** 4

Ingredients:

- 2 bell pepper, halved, seeds removed
- 4 eggs
- 1 teaspoon olive oil
- 1 pinch salt and black pepper
- 1 pinch sriracha flakes

Preparation:

1. At 390 degrees F, preheat your Air Fryer on Air Fry mode.
2. Slice the bell peppers in half, lengthwise, and remove their seeds and the inner portion to get a cup-like shape.
3. Rub olive oil on the edges of the bell peppers.
4. Place them in the Air Fryer Basket with their cut side up and crack 1 egg in each half of bell pepper.
5. Drizzle salt, black pepper, and sriracha flakes on top of the eggs.
6. Return the Air Fryer Basket to the Air Fryer and cook for 18 minutes.
7. Initiate cooking by pressing the START/PAUSE BUTTON.
8. Serve warm and fresh.

Serving Suggestion: Serve the cups with toasted bread slices and crispy bacon.

Variation Tip: Broil the cups with mozzarella cheese on top.

Nutritional Information Per Serving:

Calories 183 | Fat 15g | Sodium 402mg | Carbs 2.5g | Fiber 0.4g | Sugar 1.1g | Protein 10g

Crispy Hash Browns

Prep time: 10 minutes| **Cook time:** 13 minutes| **Serves:** 4

Ingredients:

- 3 russet potatoes
- ¼ cup chopped green peppers
- ¼ cup chopped red peppers
- ¼ cup chopped onions
- 2 garlic cloves chopped
- 1 teaspoon paprika
- Salt and black pepper, to taste
- 2 teaspoons olive oil

Preparation:

1. At 390 degrees F, preheat your Air Fryer on Air Fry mode.
2. Peel and grate all the potatoes with the help of a cheese grater.
3. Add potato shreds to a bowl filled with cold water and leave it soaked for 25 minutes.
4. Drain the water and place the potato shreds on a plate lined with a paper towel.
5. Transfer the shreds to a dry bowl and add olive oil, paprika, garlic, and black pepper.
6. Make four flat patties out of the potato mixture and place them in the Air Fryer Basket.
7. Return the Air Fryer Basket to the Air Fryer and cook for 13 minutes.
8. Initiate cooking by pressing the START/PAUSE BUTTON.
9. Flip the potato hash browns once cooked halfway through, then resume cooking.
10. Once done, serve warm.

Serving Suggestion: Serve the hash with toasted bread slices and crispy bacon.

Variation Tip: Add herbed cream on top of the hash browns.

Nutritional Information Per Serving:

Calories 190 | Fat 18g |Sodium 150mg | Carbs 0.6g | Fiber 0.4g | Sugar 0.4g | Protein 7.2g

Pumpkin Muffins

Prep time: 15 minutes| **Cook time:** 13 minutes| **Serves:** 8

Ingredients:

- ½ cup pumpkin puree
- 1 cup gluten-free oats
- ¼ cup honey
- 1 medium egg beaten
- ½ teaspoon coconut butter
- ½ tablespoons cocoa nib
- ½ tablespoons vanilla essence
- Cooking spray
- ½ teaspoon nutmeg

Preparation:

1. At 375 degrees F, preheat your Air Fryer on Air Fry mode.
2. Add oats, honey, eggs, pumpkin puree, coconut butter, cocoa nibs, vanilla essence, and nutmeg to a bowl and mix well until smooth.
3. Divide the batter into the muffin tray, greased with cooking spray.
4. Place the muffin tray in the Air Fryer Basket.
5. Return the Air Fryer Basket to the Air Fryer and cook for 13 minutes.
6. Initiate cooking by pressing the START/PAUSE BUTTON.
7. Allow the muffins to cool, then serve.

Serving Suggestion: Serve the muffins with hot coffee.

Variation Tip: Add raisins and nuts to the batter before baking.

Nutritional Information Per Serving:

Calories 209 | Fat 7.5g |Sodium 321mg | Carbs 34.1g | Fiber 4g | Sugar 3.8g | Protein 4.3g

Cinnamon Toasts

Prep time: 15 minutes | **Cook time:** 8 minutes | **Serves:** 4

Ingredients:

- 4 pieces of bread
- 2 tablespoons butter
- 2 eggs, beaten
- 1 pinch salt
- 1 pinch cinnamon ground
- 1 pinch nutmeg ground
- 1 pinch ground clove
- 1 teaspoon icing sugar

Preparation:

1. At 390 degrees F, preheat your Air Fryer on Air Fry mode.
2. Add two eggs to a mixing bowl and stir cinnamon, nutmeg, ground cloves, and salt, then whisk well.
3. Spread butter on both sides of the bread slices and cut them into thick strips.
4. Dip the breadsticks in the egg mixture and place them in the Air Fryer Basket.
5. Return the Air Fryer Basket to the Air Fryer and cook for 8 minutes.
6. Initiate cooking by pressing the START/PAUSE BUTTON.
7. Flip the French toast sticks when cooked halfway through.
8. Serve.

Serving Suggestion: Serve the toasted with chocolate syrup or Nutella spread.

Variation Tip: Use crushed cornflakes for breading to have extra crispiness.

Nutritional Information Per Serving:

Calories 199 | Fat 11.1g | Sodium 297mg | Carbs 14.9g | Fiber 1g | Sugar 2.5g | Protein 9.9g

Morning Egg Rolls

Prep time: 15 minutes| **Cook time:** 13 minutes| **Serves:** 6

Ingredients:

- 2 eggs
- 2 tablespoons milk
- Salt, to taste
- Black pepper, to taste
- ½ cup shredded cheddar cheese
- 2 sausage patties
- 6 egg roll wrappers
- 1 tablespoon olive oil
- 1 cup of water

Preparation:

1. At 375 degrees F, preheat your Air Fryer on Air Fry mode.
2. Grease a small skillet with some olive oil and place it over medium heat.
3. Add sausage patties and cook them until brown.
4. Chop the cooked patties into small pieces. Beat eggs with salt, black pepper, and milk in a mixing bowl.
5. Grease the same skillet with 1 teaspoon of olive oil and pour the egg mixture into it.
6. Stir cook to make scrambled eggs.
7. Add sausage, mix well and remove the skillet from the heat.
8. Spread an egg roll wrapper on the working surface in a diamond shape position.
9. Add a tablespoon of cheese at the bottom third of the roll wrapper.
10. Top the cheese with an egg mixture and wet the edges of the wrapper with water.
11. Fold the two corners of the wrapper and roll it, then seal the edges.
12. Repeat the same steps and place the rolls in the Air Fryer Basket.
13. Return the Air Fryer Basket to the Air Fryer and cook for 13 minutes.
14. Initiate cooking by pressing the START/PAUSE BUTTON.
15. Flip the rolls after 8 minutes and continue cooking for another 5 minutes.
16. Serve warm and fresh.

Serving Suggestion: Serve the rolls with your favorite hot sauce or cheese dip.

Variation Tip: Add crispy bacon to the filling.

Nutritional Information Per Serving:

Calories 282 | Fat 15g |Sodium 526mg | Carbs 20g | Fiber 0.6g | Sugar 3.3g | Protein 16g

Morning Patties

Prep time: 15 minutes | **Cook time:** 13 minutes | **Serves:** 4

Ingredients:

- 1 lb. minced pork
- 1 lb. minced turkey
- 2 teaspoons dry rubbed sage
- 2 teaspoons fennel seeds
- 2 teaspoons garlic powder
- 1 teaspoon paprika
- 1 teaspoon sea salt
- 1 teaspoon dried thyme

Preparation:

1. At 390 degrees F, preheat your Air Fryer on Air Fry mode.
2. In a mixing bowl, add turkey and pork, then mix them together.
3. Mix sage, fennel, paprika, salt, thyme, and garlic powder in a small bowl.
4. Drizzle this mixture over the meat mixture and mix well.
5. Take 2 tablespoons of this mixture at a time and roll it into thick patties.
6. Place the patties in the Air Fryer Basket, then spray them all with cooking oil.
7. Return the Air Fryer Basket to the Air Fryer and cook for 10 minutes.
8. Initiate cooking by pressing the START/PAUSE BUTTON.
9. Flip the patties in the basket once cooked halfway through.
10. Serve warm and fresh.

Serving Suggestion: Serve the patties with toasted bread slices.

Variation Tip: Ground chicken or beef can also be used instead of ground pork and turkey.

Nutritional Information Per Serving:

Calories 305 | Fat 25g | Sodium 532mg | Carbs 2.3g | Fiber 0.4g | Sugar 2g | Protein 18.3g

Biscuit Balls

Prep time: 10 minutes| **Cook time:** 18 minutes| **Serves:** 6

Ingredients:

- 1 tablespoon butter
- 2 eggs, beaten
- ¼ teaspoon pepper
- 1 can (10.2-oz) Pillsbury Buttermilk biscuits
- 2 ounces cheddar cheese, diced into ten cubes
- Cooking spray
- Egg Wash
- 1 egg
- 1 tablespoon water

Preparation:

1. At 375 degrees F, preheat your Air Fryer on Air Fry mode.
2. Place a suitable non-stick skillet over medium-high heat and cook the bacon until crispy, then place it on a plate lined with a paper towel.
3. Melt butter in the same skillet over medium heat. Beat eggs with pepper in a bowl and pour them into the skillet.
4. Stir cook for 5 minutes, then remove it from the heat.
5. Add bacon and mix well.
6. Divide the dough into 5 biscuits and slice each into 2 layers.
7. Press each biscuit into a 4-inch round.
8. Add a tablespoon of the egg mixture at the center of each round and top it with a piece of cheese.
9. Carefully fold the biscuit dough around the filling and pinch the edges to seal.
10. Whisk egg with water in a small bowl and brush the egg wash over the biscuits.
11. Place the biscuit bombs in the Air Fryer Basket and spray them with cooking oil.
12. Return the Air Fryer Basket to the Air Fryer and cook for 14 minutes.
13. Initiate cooking by pressing the START/PAUSE BUTTON.
14. Flip the egg bombs when cooked halfway through, then resume cooking.
15. Serve warm.

Serving Suggestion: Serve the eggs balls with crispy bacon.

Variation Tip: Add dried herbs to the egg filling.

Nutritional Information Per Serving:

Calories 102 | Fat 7.6g |Sodium 545mg | Carbs 1.5g | Fiber 0.4g | Sugar 0.7g | Protein 7.1g

Breakfast Sausage Omelet

Prep time: 10 minutes| **Cook time:** 15 minutes| **Serves:** 2

Ingredients

- ¼ pound breakfast sausage, cooked and crumbled
- 4 eggs, beaten
- ½ cup pepper Jack cheese blend
- 2 tablespoons green bell pepper, sliced
- 1 green onion, chopped
- 1 pinch cayenne pepper
- Cooking spray

Directions

1. Take a bowl and whisk eggs in it along with crumbled sausage, pepper Jack cheese, green onions, red bell pepper, and cayenne pepper.
2. Mix it all well.
3. Take cake pan that fit inside the Ninja air fryer and grease it with oil spray.
4. Pour the omelet mixture into the cake pan.
5. Preheat the unit by selecting AIR FRY mode for 3 minutes at 325 degrees F.
6. Select START/PAUSE to begin the preheating process.
7. Once preheating is done, put the cake pan inside the basket and place the basket inside the unit.
8. Turn on the Air Fry function and let it cook for 15-20 minutes at 310 degrees F.
9. Once the cooking cycle completes, take out, and serve hot, as a delicious breakfast.

Serving Suggestion: Serve it with ketchup.

Variation Tip: Use Parmesan cheese instead of pepper jack Cheese.

Nutritional Information Per Serving:

Calories 691| Fat 52.4g | Sodium1122 mg | Carbs 13.3g | Fiber 1.8g| Sugar 7g | Protein 42g

Banana and Raisins Muffins

Prep time: 20 minutes| **Cook time:** 16 minutes| **Serves:** 2

Ingredients

- Salt, pinch
- 2 eggs, whisked
- ⅓ cup butter, melted
- 4 tablespoons almond milk
- ¼ teaspoon vanilla extract
- ½ teaspoon baking powder
- 1 ½ cups all-purpose flour
- 1 cup mashed bananas
- 2 tablespoons raisins

Directions

1. Preheat the unit by selecting AIR FRY mode for 3 minutes at 325 degrees F.
2. Select START/PAUSE to begin the preheating process.
3. Once preheating is done, press START/PAUSE.
4. Take about 4 large (one-cup sized) ramekins and layer them with muffin papers.
5. Crack eggs in a large bowl, and whisk it all well and start adding vanilla extract, almond milk, baking powder, and melted butter.
6. Whisk the ingredients very well.
7. Take a separate bowl and add the all-purpose flour, and salt.
8. Now, combine the add dry ingredients with the wet ingredients.
9. Now, pour mashed bananas and raisins into this batter.
10. Mix it well to make a batter for the muffins.
11. Now pour the batter into 4 ramekins and place the ramekins in the air fryer basket.
12. Set the timer to 16 minutes at 350 degrees F at AIR FRY mode.
13. Check if not done, and let it AIR FRY for one more minute.
14. Once it is done, serve.

Serving Suggestion: None

Variation Tip: None

Nutritional Information Per Serving:

Calories 727| Fat 43.1g| Sodium366 mg | Carbs 74.4g | Fiber 4.7g | Sugar 16.1g | Protein 14.1g

Egg with Baby Spinach

Prep time: 12 minutes| **Cook time:** 12 minutes| **Serves:** 4

Ingredients

- Nonstick spray, for greasing ramekins
- 2 tablespoons olive oil
- 6 ounces baby spinach
- 2 garlic cloves, minced
- ⅓ teaspoon kosher salt
- 6-8 large eggs
- ½ cup half and half
- Salt and black pepper, to taste
- 8 Sourdough bread slices, toasted

Directions

1. Preheat the unit by selecting AIR FRY mode for 2 minutes at 350 degrees F.
2. Select START/PAUSE to begin the preheating process.
3. Once preheating is done, press START/PAUSE.
4. Grease 4 ramekins with oil spray and set aside for further use.
5. Take a skillet and heat oil in it.
6. Then cook spinach for 2 minutes and add garlic and salt black pepper.
7. Let it simmer for 2 more minutes.
8. Once the spinach is wilted, transfer it to a plate.
9. Whisk an egg into a small bowl.
10. Add in the spinach.
11. Whisk it well and then pour half and half.
12. Divide this mixture between 4 ramekins and remember not to overfill it to the top, leave a little space on top.
13. Put the ramekins in the basket of the Ninja Foodi Air Fryer.
14. Select AIR FRY mode at 350 degrees F for 12 minutes. Press START/PAUSE to initiate cooking.
15. Once it's cooked and eggs are done, serve with sourdough bread slices.

Serving Suggestion: Serve it with cream cheese topping.

Variation Tip: Use plain bread slices instead of sourdough bread slices.

Nutritional Information Per Serving:

Calories 404| Fat 19.6g| Sodium 761mg | Carbs 40.1g | Fiber 2.5g| Sugar 2.5g | Protein 19.2g

Yellow Potatoes with Eggs

Prep time: 10 minutes| **Cook time:** 30 minutes| **Serves:** 2

Ingredients

- 1 pound Dutch yellow potatoes, quartered
- 1 red bell pepper, chopped
- Salt and black pepper, to taste
- 1 green bell pepper, chopped
- 2 teaspoons olive oil
- 2 teaspoons garlic powder
- 1 teaspoon onion powder
- 1 egg
- ¼ teaspoon butter

Directions

1. Preheat the unit by selecting AIR FRY mode for 5 minutes at 325 degrees F.
2. Select START/PAUSE to begin the preheating process.
3. Toss together diced potatoes, green pepper, red pepper, salt, black pepper, and olive oil along with garlic powder and onion powder.
4. Take ramekin and grease it with oil spray.
5. Whisk egg in a bowl and add salt and pepper along with ½ teaspoon of butter.
6. Pour egg into a ramekin and place ramekins inside the air fryer.
7. Transfer bowl ingredients to the air fryer basket aside the ramekins.
8. Set the timer for basket to 30 minutes at 400 degrees F, on the AIR FRY mode.
9. Once preheating is done, press START/PAUSE.
10. Once 10 minutes pass, press START/PAUSE and takeout the ramekin.
11. Press the START/PAUSE button, and let the potato cook for remaining minutes.
12. Once done, serve and enjoy.

Serving Suggestion: Serve it with sourdough toasted bread slices.

Variation Tip: Use white potatoes instead of yellow Dutch potatoes.

Nutritional Information Per Serving:

Calories252 | Fat 7.5g | Sodium 37mg | Carbs 40g | Fiber3.9g | Sugar 7g | Protein 6.7g

Snacks and Appetizers Recipes

Onion Rings

Prep time: 10 minutes| **Cook time:** 22 minutes| **Serves:** 4

Ingredients:

- ¾ cup all-purpose flour
- 1 teaspoon salt
- 1 large onion, cut into rings
- ½ cup cornstarch
- 2 teaspoons baking powder
- 1 cup low-fat milk
- 1 egg
- 1 cup bread crumbs
- ⅙ teaspoons paprika
- Cooking spray
- ⅙ teaspoons garlic powder

Preparation:

1. At 375 degrees F, preheat your Air Fryer on Air Fry mode.
2. Mix flour with baking powder, cornstarch, and salt in a small bowl.
3. First, coat the onion rings with flour mixture; set them aside.
4. Beat milk with egg, then add the remaining flour mixture into the egg.
5. Mix them well together to make a thick batter.
6. Now dip the floured onion rings into the prepared batter and coat them well.
7. Place the rings on a wire rack for 10 minutes.
8. Spread bread crumbs in a shallow bowl.
9. Coat the onion rings with breadcrumbs and shake off the excess.
10. Set the coated onion rings in the Air Fryer Basket.
11. Spray all the rings with the cooking spray.
12. Return the Air Fryer Basket to the Air Fryer and cook for 22 minutes.
13. Initiate cooking by pressing the START/PAUSE BUTTON.
14. Flip once cooked halfway through, then resume cooking
15. Season the air fried onion rings with garlic powder and paprika.
16. Serve.

Serving Suggestion: Serve with tomato sauce or cream cheese dip.

Variation Tip: Use crushed cornflakes for breading to have extra crispiness.

Nutritional Information Per Serving:
Calories 229 | Fat 1.9 |Sodium 567mg | Carbs 1.9g | Fiber 0.4g | Sugar 0.6g | Protein 11.8g

Crispy Tortilla Chips

Prep time: 15 minutes| **Cook time:** 13 minutes| **Serves:** 8

Ingredients:
- 4 (6-inch) corn tortillas
- 1 tablespoon avocado oil
- Sea salt to taste
- Cooking spray

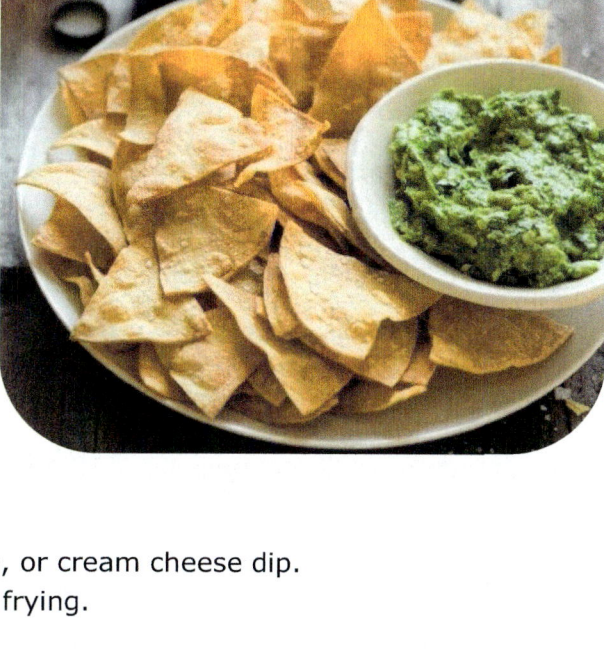

Preparation:

1. At 390 degrees F, preheat your Air Fryer on Air Fry mode.
2. Spread the corn tortillas on the working surface.
3. Slice them into bite-sized triangles.
4. Toss them with salt and cooking oil.
5. Place the triangles in the Air Fryer Basket in a single layer.
6. Return the Air Fryer Basket to the Air Fryer and cook for 13 minutes.
7. Initiate cooking by pressing the START/PAUSE BUTTON.
8. Toss the chips once cooked halfway through, then resume cooking.
9. Serve and enjoy.

Serving Suggestion: Serve with guacamole, mayonnaise, or cream cheese dip.

Variation Tip: Drizzle parmesan cheese on top before air frying.

Nutritional Information Per Serving:

Calories 103 | Fat 8.4g |Sodium 117mg | Carbs 3.5g | Fiber 0.9g | Sugar 1.5g | Protein 5.1g

Parmesan French Fries

Prep time: 10 minutes| **Cook time:** 20 minutes| **Serves:** 6

Ingredients:
- 3 medium russet potatoes
- 2 tablespoons parmesan cheese
- 2 tablespoons fresh parsley, chopped
- 1 tablespoon olive oil
- Salt, to taste

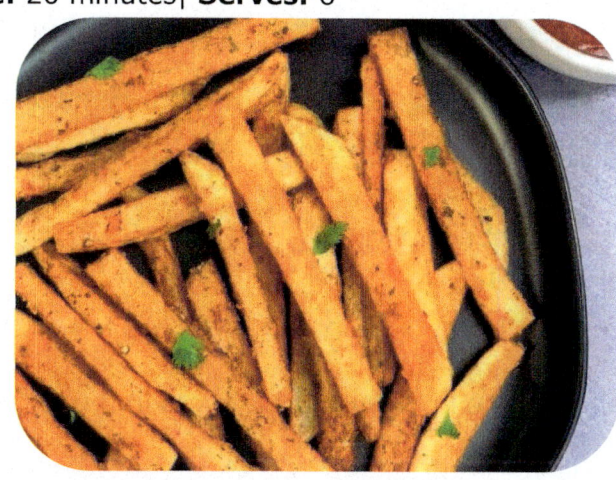

Preparation:

1. At 360 degrees F, preheat your Air Fryer on Air Fry mode.
2. Wash the potatoes and pass them through the fries' cutter to get ¼-inch-thick fries.
3. Place the fries in a colander and drizzle salt on top.
4. Leave these fries for 10 minutes, then rinse.
5. Toss the potatoes with parmesan cheese, oil, salt, and parsley in a bowl.
6. Place the potatoes into the Air Fryer Basket.
7. Return the Air Fryer Basket to the Air Fryer and cook for 20 minutes.
8. Initiate cooking by pressing the START/PAUSE BUTTON.
9. Toss the chips once cooked halfway through, then resume cooking.
10. Serve warm.

Serving Suggestion: Serve with tomato ketchup, Asian coleslaw, or creamed cabbage.

Variation Tip: Toss fries with black pepper for change of taste.

Nutritional Information Per Serving:

Calories 307 | Fat 8.6g |Sodium 510mg | Carbs 22.2g | Fiber 1.4g | Sugar 13g | Protein 33.6g

Stuffed Bell Peppers

Prep time: 25 minutes| **Cook time:** 16 minutes| **Serves:** 3

Ingredients

- 6 large bell peppers
- 1 ½ cups cooked rice
- 2 cups cheddar cheese

Directions

1. Preheat the unit by selecting AIR FRY mode for 5 minutes at 350 degrees F.
2. Select START/PAUSE to begin the preheating process.
3. Once preheating is done, press START/PAUSE.
4. Cut the bell peppers in half lengthwise and remove all the seeds.
5. Fill the cavity of each bell pepper with cooked rice.
6. Grease the basket of air fryer with oil spray
7. Transfer the bell peppers to the basket of the Ninja Air Fryer.
8. Set the time for 200 degrees F for 10 minutes.
9. Afterward, take out the basket and sprinkle cheese on top.
10. Set the time at 200 degrees F for 6 minutes.
11. Once it's done, serve.

Serving Suggestion: Serve it with mashed potato.

Variation Tip: You can use any cheese you like.

Nutritional Information Per Serving:
Calories 605| Fat 26g | Sodium477 mg | Carbs68.3 g | Fiber4 g| Sugar 12.5g | Protein25.6 g

Fried Halloumi Cheese

Prep time: 10 minutes| **Cook time:** 12 minutes| **Serves:** 6

Ingredients:

- 1 block halloumi cheese, sliced
- 2 teaspoons olive oil

Preparation:

1. At 360 degrees F, preheat your Air Fryer on Air Fry mode.
2. Place the halloumi cheese slices in the Air Fryer Basket.
3. Drizzle olive oil over the cheese slices.
4. Return the Air Fryer Basket to the Air Fryer and cook for 12 minutes.
5. Flip the cheese slices once cooked halfway through.
6. Serve.

Serving Suggestion: Serve with fresh yogurt dip or cucumber salad.

Variation Tip: Add black pepper and salt for seasoning.

Nutritional Information Per Serving:
Calories 186 | Fat 3g |Sodium 223mg | Carbs 31g | Fiber 8.7g | Sugar 5.5g | Protein 9.7g

Sweet Bites

Prep time: 25 minutes| **Cook time:** 10 minutes| **Serves:** 4

Ingredients

- 10 sheets of Phyllo dough, (filo dough)
- 2 tablespoons melted butter
- 1 cup walnuts, chopped
- 2 teaspoons honey
- 1 Pinch cinnamon
- 1 teaspoon orange zest

Directions

1. Preheat the unit by selecting AIR FRY mode for 2 minutes at 325 degrees F.
2. Select START/PAUSE to begin the preheating process.
3. Once preheating is done, press START/PAUSE.
4. First, layer together 10 Phyllo dough sheets on a flat surface.
5. Then cut it into 4*4-inch squares.
6. Now, coat the squares with butter, drizzle some honey, orange zest, walnuts, and cinnamon.
7. Bring all 4 corners together and press the corners to make a little like purse design.
8. Put it inside the air fryer basket and select the AIR FRY mode and set it for 10 minutes at 375 degrees F.
9. Once done, take out and serve.

Serving Suggestion: Serve with a topping of nuts.

Variation Tip: None.

Nutritional Information Per Serving:
Calories 397| Fat 27.1 g| Sodium 271mg | Carbs31.2 g | Fiber 3.2g| Sugar3.3g | Protein 11g

Peppered Asparagus

Prep time: 10 minutes| **Cook time:** 16 minutes| **Serves:** 6

Ingredients:

- 1 bunch of asparagus, trimmed
- Avocado or olive oil
- Himalayan salt, to taste
- Black pepper, to taste

Preparation:

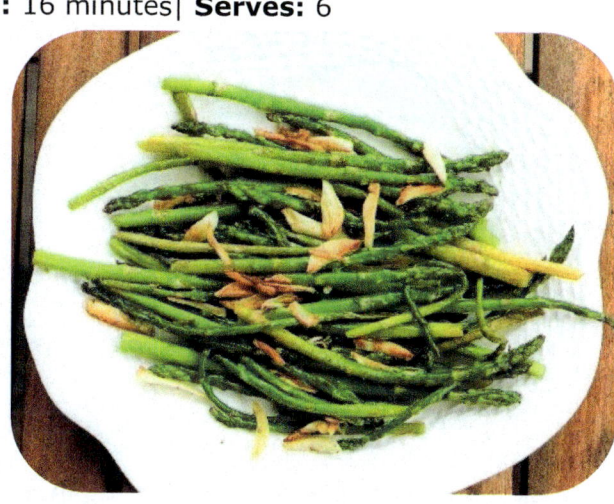

1. At 390 degrees F, preheat your Air Fryer on Air Fry mode.
2. Place the asparagus in the Air Fryer Basket.
3. Toss the asparagus with salt, black pepper, and oil.
4. Return the Air Fryer Basket to the Air Fryer and cook for 16 minutes.
5. Initiate cooking by pressing the START/PAUSE BUTTON.
6. Serve warm.

Serving Suggestion: Serve with mayonnaise or cream cheese dip.

Variation Tip: Use panko crumbs for breading to have extra crispiness.

Nutritional Information Per Serving:
Calories 163 | Fat 11.5g |Sodium 918mg | Carbs 8.3g | Fiber 4.2g | Sugar 0.2g | Protein 7.4g

Cheddar Quiche

Prep time: 10 minutes| **Cook time:** 12 minutes| **Serves:** 2

Ingredients
- 4 eggs, organic
- 1 ¼ cups heavy cream
- Salt, pinch
- ½ cup broccoli florets
- ½ cup cheddar cheese, shredded and for sprinkling

Directions
1. Take a Pyrex pitcher and crack two eggs in it.
2. And fill it with heavy cream, about half the way up.
3. Add in the salt and then add in the broccoli and pour this into a quiche dish, and top it with shredded cheddar cheese.
4. Preheat the unit by selecting AIR FRY mode for 2 minutes at 325 degrees F.
5. Select START/PAUSE to begin the preheating process.
6. Once preheating is done, press START/PAUSE.
7. Now put the dish inside air fryer basket.
8. Set the time to 12 minutes at 325 degrees F.
9. Once done, serve hot.

Serving Suggestion: Serve with herbs as a topping.
Variation Tip: Use spinach instead of broccoli florets.
Nutritional Information Per Serving:
Calories 454| Fat40g | Sodium 406mg | Carbs 4.2g | Fiber 0.6g| Sugar1.3 g | Protein 20g

Crispy Plantain Chips

Prep time: 15 minutes| **Cook time:** 20 minutes| **Serves:** 4

Ingredients:
- 1 green plantain
- 1 teaspoon canola oil
- ½ teaspoons sea salt

Preparation:
1. At 350 degrees F, preheat your Air Fryer on Air Fry mode.
2. Peel and cut the plantains into long strips using a mandolin slicer.
3. Grease the Air Fryer Basket with a ½ teaspoon with canola oil.
4. Toss the plantains with salt and remaining canola oil.
5. Place these plantains in the Air Fryer Basket.
6. Return the Air Fryer Basket to the Air Fryer and cook for 20 minutes.
7. Toss the plantains after 10 minutes and resume cooking.
8. Serve warm.

Serving Suggestion: Serve with cream cheese dip and celery sticks.
Variation Tip: Use black pepper to season the chips.
Nutritional Information Per Serving:
Calories 122 | Fat 1.8g |Sodium 794mg | Carbs 17g | Fiber 8.9g | Sugar 1.6g | Protein 14.9g

Grill Cheese Sandwich

Prep time: 15 minutes | **Cook time:** 10 minutes | **Serves:** 2

Ingredients

- 4 slices white bread slices
- 2 tablespoons of butter, melted
- 2 slices sharp cheddar
- 2 slices Swiss cheese
- 2 slices mozzarella cheese

Directions

1. Preheat the unit by selecting AIR FRY mode for 2 minutes at 325 degrees F.
2. Select START/PAUSE to begin the preheating process.
3. Once preheating is done, press START/PAUSE.
4. Brush melted butter on one side of all the bread slices and then top the 2 bread slices with slices of cheddar, Swiss, and mozzarella, one slice per bread.
5. Top it with the other slice to make a sandwich.
6. Add it to the basket of the air fryer.
7. Turn on AIR FRY mode at 350 degrees F for 10 minutes.
8. Once done, serve.

Serving Suggestion: Serve with tomato soup.

Variation Tip: Use oil spray instead of butter.

Nutritional Information Per Serving:
Calories 577 | Fat38g | Sodium 1466mg | Carbs 30.5g | Fiber 1.1g | Sugar 6.5g | Protein 27.6g

Chicken Crescent Wraps

Prep time: 10 minutes | **Cook time:** 12 minutes | **Serves:** 6

Ingredients:

- 3 tablespoons chopped onion
- 3 garlic cloves, peeled and minced
- ¾ (8 ounces) package cream cheese
- 6 tablespoons butter
- 2 boneless chicken breasts, cubed, cooked
- 3 (10 ounces) cans of refrigerated crescent roll dough

Preparation:

1. At 390 degrees F, preheat your Air Fryer on Air Fry mode.
2. Heat oil in a skillet and add onion and garlic to sauté until soft.
3. Add cooked chicken, sautéed veggies, butter, and cream cheese to a blender.
4. Blend well until smooth. Spread the crescent dough over a flat surface.
5. Slice the dough into 12 rectangles.
6. Spoon the chicken mixture at the center of each rectangle.
7. Roll the dough to wrap the mixture and form a ball.
8. Place these balls in the Air Fryer Basket.
9. Return the Air Fryer Basket to the Air Fryer and cook for 12 minutes.
10. Initiate cooking by pressing the START/PAUSE BUTTON.
11. Serve warm.

Serving Suggestion: Serve with tomato sauce or cream cheese dip.

Variation Tip: You can also prepare the filling using leftover turkey or pork.

Nutritional Information Per Serving:
Calories 100 | Fat 2g | Sodium 480mg | Carbs 4g | Fiber 2g | Sugar 0g | Protein 18g

Blueberries Muffins

Prep time: 15 minutes| **Cook time:** 15 minutes| **Serves:** 2

Ingredients

- Salt, pinch
- 2 eggs
- ⅓ cup sugar
- ⅓ cup vegetable oil
- 4 tablespoons water
- 1 teaspoon lemon zest
- ¼ teaspoon vanilla extract
- ½ teaspoon baking powder
- 1 cup all-purpose flour
- 1 cup blueberries

Directions

1. Take 4 one-cup sized ramekins that are oven safe and layer them with muffin papers.
2. Take a bowl and whisk the egg, sugar, oil, water, vanilla extract, and lemon zest.
3. Whisk it all very well.
4. Now, in a separate bowl, mix the flour, baking powder, and salt.
5. Now, add dry ingredients slowly to wet ingredients.
6. Now, pour this batter into ramekins and top it with blueberries.
7. Preheat the unit by selecting AIR FRY mode for 2 minutes at 325 degrees F.
8. Select START/PAUSE to begin the preheating process.
9. Once preheating is done, press START/PAUSE.
10. Now, place the ramekins inside the Ninja Foodi Air Fryer.
11. Set the time to AIR FRY mode for 15 minutes at 350 degrees F.
12. Check if not done, and let it AIR FRY for one more minute.
13. Once it is done, serve.

Serving Suggestion: Serve it with whipped cream topping.

Variation Tip: Use butter instead of vegetable oil.

Nutritional Information Per Serving:

Calories 781| Fat41.6g | Sodium 143mg | Carbs 92.7g | Fiber 3.5g| Sugar41.2 g | Protein 0g

Chicken Tenders

Prep time: 15 minutes | **Cook time:** 12 minutes | **Serves:** 3

Ingredients

- 1 pound chicken tender
- Salt and black pepper, to taste
- 1 cup Panko bread crumbs
- 2 cups Italian bread crumbs
- 1 cup parmesan cheese
- 2 eggs
- Oil spray, for greasing

Directions

1. Sprinkle the tenders with salt and black pepper.
2. In a medium bowl, mix Panko bread crumbs with Italian breadcrumbs.
3. Add salt, pepper, and parmesan cheese.
4. Crack two eggs in a bowl.
5. First, put the chicken tender in eggs.
6. Now dredge the tender in a bowl and coat the tender well with crumbs.
7. Preheat the unit by selecting AIR FRY mode for 2 minutes at 325 degrees F.
8. Select START/PAUSE to begin the preheating process.
9. Once preheating is done, press START/PAUSE.
10. Line the basket of the air fryer with parchment paper.
11. At the end, spray the tenders with oil spray.
12. Layer the tenders inside the basket of Ninja Foodi Air Fryer.
13. Set it to the AIR FRY mode at 350 degrees F for 12 minutes.
14. Once it's done, serve.

Serving Suggestion: Serve it with ranch or ketchup.

Variation Tip: Use Italian seasoning instead of Italian bread crumbs.

Nutritional Information Per Serving:

Calories558 | Fat23.8g | Sodium872 mg | Carbs 20.9g | Fiber1.7 g| Sugar2.2 g | Protein 63.5g

Beef, Lamb and Pork Recipes

Zucchini Pork Skewers

Prep time: 15 minutes | **Cook time:** 23 minutes | **Serves:** 4

Ingredients:

- 1 large zucchini, cut 1" pieces
- 1 lb. boneless pork belly, cut into cubes
- 1 onion yellow, diced in squares
- 1 ½ cups grape tomatoes
- 1 garlic clove minced
- 1 lemon, juice only
- ¼ cup olive oil
- 2 tablespoons balsamic vinegar
- 1 teaspoon oregano
- olive oil spray

Preparation:

1. At 390 degrees F, preheat your Air Fryer on Air Fry mode.
2. Mix together balsamic vinegar, garlic, oregano lemon juice, and ¼ cup of olive oil in a suitable bowl.
3. Then toss in diced pork pieces and mix well to coat.
4. Leave the seasoned pork to marinate for 60 minutes in the refrigerator.
5. Take suitable wooden skewers for your Air Fryer's Basket, and then thread marinated pork and vegetables on each skewer in an alternating manner.
6. Place the skewers in the Air Fryer Basket and spray them with cooking oil.
7. Return the Air Fryer Basket to the Air Fryer and cook for 23 minutes.
8. Initiate cooking by pressing the START/PAUSE BUTTON.
9. Flip the skewers once cooked halfway through, and resume cooking.
10. Serve warm.

Serving Suggestion: Serve with sautéed green beans and cherry tomatoes.

Variation Tip: Use honey glaze to baste the skewers.

Nutritional Information Per Serving:
Calories 459 | Fat 17.7g | Sodium 1516mg | Carbs 1.7g | Fiber 0.5g | Sugar 0.4g | Protein 69.2g

Beef Cheeseburgers

Prep time: 15 minutes| **Cook time:** 13 minutes| **Serves:** 4

Ingredients:

- 1 lb. ground beef
- Salt, to taste
- 2 garlic cloves, minced
- 1 tablespoon soy sauce
- Black pepper, to taste
- 4 American cheese slices
- 4 hamburger buns
- Mayonnaise, to serve
- Lettuce, to serve
- Sliced tomatoes, to serve
- Sliced red onion, to serve

Preparation:

1. At 390 degrees F, preheat your Air Fryer on Air Fry mode.
2. Mix beef with soy sauce and garlic in a large bowl.
3. Make 4 patties of 4 inches in diameter.
4. Rub them with salt and black pepper on both sides.
5. Place the patties in the Air Fryer Basket.
6. Return the Air Fryer Basket to the Air Fryer and cook for 13 minutes.
7. Initiate cooking by pressing the START/PAUSE BUTTON.
8. Flip each patty once cooked halfway through, and resume cooking.
9. Add each patty to the hamburger buns along with mayo, tomatoes, onions, and lettuce.
10. Serve.

Serving Suggestion: Serve with tomato ketchup or chili sauce.

Variation Tip: Add breadcrumbs to the beef burger mixture for a crumbly texture.

Nutritional Information Per Serving:

Calories 437 | Fat 28g |Sodium 1221mg | Carbs 22.3g | Fiber 0.9g | Sugar 8g | Protein 30.3g

Gochujang Brisket

Prep time: 20 minutes | **Cook time:** 55 minutes | **Serves:** 6

Ingredients:

- ½ tablespoon sweet paprika
- ½ teaspoon toasted sesame oil
- 2 lbs. beef brisket, cut into 4 pieces
- Salt, to taste
- ⅛ cup Gochujang, Korean chili paste
- Black pepper, to taste
- 1 small onion, diced
- 2 garlic cloves, minced
- 1 teaspoon Asian fish sauce
- 1 ½ tablespoons peanut oil, as needed
- ½ tablespoons fresh ginger, grated
- ¼ teaspoon red chili flakes
- ½ cup water
- 1 tablespoon ketchup
- 1 tablespoon soy sauce

Preparation:

1. At 390 degrees F, preheat your Air Fryer on Air Fry mode.
2. Thoroughly rub the beef brisket with olive oil, paprika, chili flakes, black pepper, and salt.
3. Place the brisket in the Air Fryer Basket.
4. Return the Air Fryer Basket to the Air Fryer and cook for 35 minutes.
5. Initiate cooking by pressing the START/PAUSE BUTTON.
6. Flip the brisket halfway through, and resume cooking.
7. Meanwhile, heat oil in a skillet and add ginger, onion, and garlic.
8. Sauté for 5 minutes, then add all the remaining ingredients.
9. Cook the mixture for 15 minutes approximately until well thoroughly mixed.
10. Serve the brisket with this sauce on top.

Serving Suggestion: Serve on top of boiled white rice.

Variation Tip: Add Worcestershire sauce and honey to taste.

Nutritional Information Per Serving:

Calories 374 | Fat 25g | Sodium 275mg | Carbs 7.3g | Fiber 0g | Sugar 6g | Protein 12.3g

Chipotle Beef

Prep time: 15 minutes| **Cook time:** 18 minutes| **Serves:** 4

Ingredients:

- 1 lb. beef steak, cut into chunks
- 1 large egg
- ½ cup parmesan cheese, grated
- ½ cup pork panko
- ½ teaspoon seasoned salt

Chipotle Ranch Dip

- ¼ cup mayonnaise
- ¼ cup sour cream
- 1 teaspoon chipotle paste
- ½ teaspoon ranch dressing mix
- ¼ medium lime, juiced

Preparation:

1. At 390 degrees F, preheat your Air Fryer on Air Fry mode.
2. Mix all the ingredients for chipotle ranch dip in a bowl.
3. Keep it in the refrigerator for 30 minutes.
4. Mix pork panko with salt and parmesan.
5. Beat egg in one bowl and spread the panko mixture in another flat bowl.
6. Dip the steak chunks in the egg first, then coat them with panko mixture.
7. Spread them in the Air Fryer Basket and spray them with cooking oil.
8. Return the Air Fryer Basket to the Air Fryer and cook for 18 minutes.
9. Initiate cooking by pressing the START/PAUSE BUTTON.
10. Serve with chipotle ranch and salt and pepper on top. Enjoy.

Serving Suggestion: Serve with tomato ketchup or chili sauce.

Variation Tip: Add crushed cornflakes for breading to get extra crisp.

Nutritional Information Per Serving:

Calories 310 | Fat 17g |Sodium 271mg | Carbs 4.3g | Fiber 0.9g | Sugar 2.1g | Protein 35g

Mustard Rubbed Lamb Chops

Prep time: 15 minutes | **Cook time:** 32 minutes | **Serves:** 4

Ingredients:

- 1 teaspoon Dijon mustard
- 1 teaspoon olive oil
- ½ teaspoon soy sauce
- ½ teaspoon garlic, minced
- ½ teaspoon cumin powder
- ½ teaspoon cayenne pepper
- ½ teaspoon Italian spice blend
- ⅛ teaspoon salt
- 4 pieces of lamb chops

Preparation:

1. At 350 degrees F, preheat your Air Fryer on Air Fry mode.
2. Mix Dijon mustard, soy sauce, olive oil, garlic, cumin powder, cayenne pepper, Italian spice blend, and salt in a medium bowl and mix well.
3. Place lamb chops into a Ziploc bag and pour in the marinade.
4. Press the air out of the bag and seal tightly.
5. Press the marinade around the lamb chops to coat.
6. Keep then in the fridge and marinate for at least 30 minutes, up to overnight.
7. Place the chops in the Air Fryer Basket and spray them with cooking oil.
8. Return the Air Fryer Basket to the Air Fryer and cook for 27 minutes.
9. Initiate cooking by pressing the START/PAUSE BUTTON.
10. Flip the chops once cooked halfway through, and resume cooking.
11. Switch the Air fryer to AIR broil mode and cook for 5 minutes.
12. Serve warm.

Serving Suggestion: Serve the chops with a dollop of cream cheese dip on top.

Variation Tip: Rub the lamb chops with balsamic vinegar or honey before seasoning.

Nutritional Information Per Serving:

Calories 264 | Fat 17g | Sodium 129mg | Carbs 0.9g | Fiber 0.3g | Sugar 0g | Protein 27g

Lamb Shank with Mushroom Sauce

Prep time: 15 minutes| **Cook time:** 35 minutes| **Serves:** 4

Ingredients:

- 20 mushrooms, chopped
- 2 red bell pepper, chopped
- 2 red onion, chopped
- 1 cup red wine
- 4 leeks, chopped
- 6 tablespoons balsamic vinegar
- 2 teaspoons black pepper
- 2 teaspoons salt
- 3 tablespoons fresh rosemary
- 6 garlic cloves
- 4 lamb shanks
- 3 tablespoons olive oil

Preparation:

1. At 390 degrees F, preheat your Air Fryer on Air Fry mode.
2. Season the lamb shanks with salt, pepper, rosemary, and 1 teaspoon of olive oil.
3. Set the shanks in the Air Fryer Basket.
4. Return the Air Fryer Basket to the Air Fryer and cook for 25 minutes.
5. Initiate cooking by pressing the START/PAUSE BUTTON.
6. Flip the shanks halfway through, and resume cooking.
7. Meanwhile, add and heat the remaining olive oil in a skillet.
8. Add onion and garlic to sauté for 5 minutes.
9. Add in mushrooms and cook for 5 minutes.
10. Add red wine and cook until it is absorbed
11. Stir all the remaining vegetables along with black pepper and salt.
12. Cook until vegetables are al dente.
13. Serve the air fried shanks with sautéed vegetable fry.

Serving Suggestion: Serve with sautéed zucchini and green beans.

Variation Tip: Rub the lamb shanks with lemon juice before seasoning.

Nutritional Information Per Serving:

Calories 352 | Fat 9.1g |Sodium 1294mg | Carbs 3.9g | Fiber 1g | Sugar 1g | Protein 61g

Ham Burger Patties

Prep time: 15 minutes | **Cook time:** 16 minutes | **Serves:** 2

Ingredients

- 1 pound ground beef
- Salt and pepper, to taste
- ½ teaspoon red chili powder
- ¼ teaspoon coriander powder
- 2 tablespoons chopped onion
- 1 green chili, chopped
- Oil spray for greasing
- 2 large potato wedges

Directions

1. Take out the rack and oil greases the air fryer basket with oil spray.
2. Add potato wedges in the basket.
3. Put the rack on top and cover it with aluminum foil.
4. Take a bowl and add minced beef in it and add salt, pepper, chili powder, coriander powder, green chili, and chopped onion.
5. Mix well and make two burger patties with wet hands.
6. Put the patties beside wedges inside air fryer.
7. Now, set time for 12 minutes using AIR FRY mode at 400 degrees F.
8. Once the time of cooking complete, take out the basket.
9. Flip the patties and turn and twist the potatoes wedges.
10. Again, set the air fryer for 4 minutes at 400 degrees F.
11. Once it's done, serve and enjoy.

Serving Suggestion: Serve it with bread slices, cheese, and pickles, lettuce, and onion.

Variation Tip: None.

Nutritional Information Per Serving: Calories875 | Fat21.5g | Sodium 622mg | Carbs 88g | Fiber10.9 g| Sugar 3.4g | Protein 78.8g

Bell Peppers with Sausages

Prep time: 15 minutes| **Cook time:** 15 minutes| **Serves:** 4

Ingredients

- 6 beef or pork Italian sausages
- 4 bell peppers, whole
- Oil spray, for greasing
- 2 cups cooked rice
- 1 cup sour cream

Directions

1. Preheat the unit by selecting AIR FRY mode for 2 minutes at 325 degrees F.
2. Select START/PAUSE to begin the preheating process.
3. Once preheating is done, press START/PAUSE.
4. Put the bell pepper inside the basket and sausages accommodating aside.
5. Now, place the basket inside the unit.
6. Set it to AIR FRY mode for 15 minutes at 400 degrees F.
7. Once done and serve over cooked rice with a dollop of sour cream.

Serving Suggestion: Serve it with salad.

Variation Tip: Use olive oil instead of oil spray.

Nutritional Information Per Serving:
Calories1356 | Fat 81.2g| Sodium 3044 mg | Carbs 96g | Fiber 3.1g | Sugar 8.3g | Protein 57.2 g

Parmesan Pork Chops

Prep time: 10 minutes| **Cook time:** 15 minutes| **Serves:** 4

Ingredients:

- 4 boneless pork chops
- 2 tablespoons olive oil
- ½ cup freshly grated Parmesan
- 1 teaspoon salt
- 1 teaspoon paprika
- 1 teaspoon garlic powder
- 1 teaspoon onion powder
- ½ teaspoon black pepper

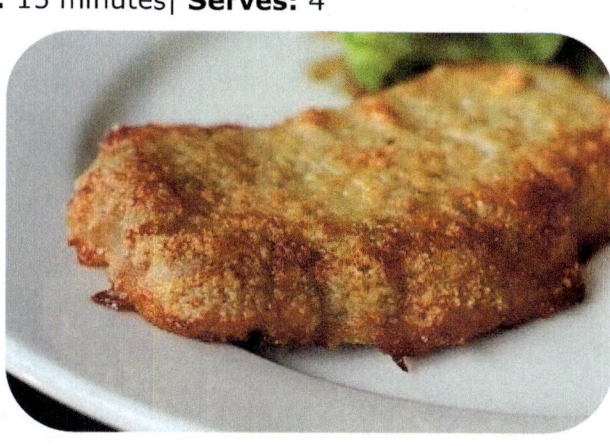

Preparation:

1. At 390 degrees F, preheat your Air Fryer on Air Fry mode.
2. Pat dry the pork chops with a paper towel and rub them with olive oil.
3. Mix parmesan with spices in a medium bowl.
4. Rub the pork chops with Parmesan mixture.
5. Place the seasoned pork chops in the Air Fryer Basket.
6. Return the Air Fryer Basket to the Air Fryer and cook for 15 minutes.
7. Initiate cooking by pressing the START/PAUSE BUTTON.
8. Flip the pork chops when cooked halfway through, then resume cooking.
9. Serve warm.

Serving Suggestion: Serve boiled rice or steamed cauliflower rice.

Variation Tip: Rub the chops with garlic cloves before seasoning.

Nutritional Information Per Serving:
Calories 396 | Fat 23.2g |Sodium 622mg | Carbs 0.7g | Fiber 0g | Sugar 0g | Protein 45.6g

Short Ribs & Root Vegetables

Prep time: 15 minutes | **Cook time:** 45 minutes | **Serves:** 2

Ingredients

- 1 pound beef short ribs, bone-in and trimmed
- Salt and black pepper, to taste
- 2 tablespoons canola oil, divided
- ¼ cup red wine
- 3 tablespoons brown sugar
- 2 cloves garlic, peeled, minced
- 4 carrots, peeled, cut into 1-inch pieces
- 2 parsnips, peeled, cut into 1-inch pieces
- ½ cup pearl onions

Directions

1. Preheat the unit by selecting AIR FRY mode for 5 minutes at 325 degrees F.
2. Select START/PAUSE to begin the preheating process.
3. Once preheating is done, press START/PAUSE.
4. Season the ribs with salt and black pepper and rub a little amount of canola oil on both sides.
5. Place it in the basket of the air fryer.
6. Next, take a bowl and add pearl onions, parsnip, carrots, garlic, brown sugar, red wine, salt, and black pepper.
7. Add the vegetable mixture over the ribs.
8. Set the time to 45 minutes at 390 degrees F on AIR FRY mode.
9. Hit START/PAUSE so the cooking cycle being.
10. Once the cooking complete, take out the ingredient and serve short ribs with the mixed vegetables and liquid collect at the bottom of basket.
11. Enjoy it hot.

Serving Suggestion: Serve it with mashed potatoes.

Variation Tip: Use olive oil instead of canola oil.

Nutritional Information Per Serving:

Calories1262 | Fat 98.6g| Sodium 595mg | Carbs 57g | Fiber 10.1g| Sugar 28.2g | Protein 35.8g

Chinese BBQ Pork

Prep time: 15 minutes| **Cook time:** 25-40 minutes| **Serves:** 2

Sauce Ingredients

- 4 tablespoons soy sauce
- ¼ cup red wine
- 2 tablespoons oyster sauce
- ¼ tablespoons hoisin sauce
- ¼ cup honey
- ¼ cup brown sugar
- 1 Pinch salt
- 1 Pinch black pepper
- 1 teaspoon ginger garlic, paste
- 1 teaspoon five-spice powder

Other Ingredients

- 1.5 pounds pork shoulder, sliced

Directions

1. Take a bowl and mix all the ingredients listed under sauce ingredients.
2. Transfer half of it to a sauce pan and let it cook for 10 minutes.
3. Set it aside.
4. Let the pork marinate in the remaining sauce for 2 hours.
5. Afterward, put the pork slices in the basket and set it to AIR FRY mode 400 degrees F for 30 minutes.
6. Make sure the internal temperature is above 160 degrees F once cooked.
7. If not add a few more minutes to the overall cooking time.
8. Once done, take it out and baste it with prepared sauce.
9. Serve and Enjoy.

Serving Suggestion: Serve it with rice.

Variation Tip: Skip the wine and add vinegar.

Nutritional Information Per Serving:

Calories 1239| Fat 73 g| Sodium 2185 mg | Carbs 57.3 g | Fiber 0.4g| Sugar53.7 g | Protein 81.5 g

Pork Chops

Prep time: 10 minutes| **Cook time:** 20 minutes| **Serves:** 2

Ingredients

- 1 tablespoon rosemary, chopped
- Salt and black pepper, to taste
- 2 garlic cloves
- 1 inch ginger
- 2 tablespoons olive oil
- 8 pork chops

Directions

1. Take a blender and pulse together rosemary, salt, pepper, garlic cloves, ginger, and olive oil.
2. Rub this marinade over pork chops and let it rest for 1 hour.
3. Then adjust it inside the air fryer and set it to AIR FRY mode for 20 minutes at 375 degrees F.
4. Once the cooking cycle is done, take out and serve hot.

Serving Suggestion: Serve it with salad.

Variation Tip: Use canola oil instead of olive oil.

Nutritional Information Per Serving:

Calories 1154| Fat 93.8g| Sodium 225mg | Carbs 2.1g | Fiber0.8 g| Sugar 0g | Protein 72.2g

Steak and Mashed Creamy Potatoes

Prep time: 15 minutes | **Cook time:** 45-50 minutes | **Serves:** 1

Ingredients

- 2 Russet potatoes, peeled and cubed
- ¼ cup butter, divided
- ⅓ cup heavy cream
- ½ cup shredded cheddar cheese
- Salt and black pepper, to taste
- 1 New York strip steak, about a pound
- 1 teaspoon olive oil
- Oil spray, for greasing

Directions

1. Preheat the unit by selecting AIR FRY mode for 5 minutes at 350 degrees F.
2. Select START/PAUSE to begin the preheating process.
3. Once preheating is done, press START/PAUSE.
4. Rub the potatoes with salt and a little amount of olive oil about a teaspoon.
5. Next, season the steak with salt and black pepper.
6. Place the russet potatoes along with steak in basket of air fryer.
7. Oil sprays the steak and set it to AIR FRY mode for 50 minutes, at 375 degrees F.
8. Hit START/PAUSE and let the Ninja Foodi do its magic.
9. One 12 minutes pass, take out the steak and let the cooking cycle completes.
10. Afterward take out potato and mash the potatoes and then add butter, heavy cream, and cheese along with salt and black pepper.
11. Serve the mashed potatoes with steak.
12. Enjoy.

Serving Suggestion: Serve it with rice.

Variation Tip: Use Parmesan instead of cheddar.

Nutritional Information Per Serving:
Calories1932 | Fat 85.2g | Sodium 3069mg | Carbs 82g | Fiber10.3 g | Sugar 5.3g | Protein 22.5g

Steak in Air Fry

Prep time: 15 minutes| **Cook time:** 22 minutes| **Serves:** 1

Ingredients

- 2 teaspoons canola oil
- 1 tablespoon Montreal steaks seasoning
- 1 pound beef steak

Directions

1. Season the steak on both sides with canola oil and then rub a generous amount of steak seasoning all over.
2. Put the steak in the basket and set it to AIR FRY mode at 400 degrees F for 22 minutes.
3. After 7 minutes, hit pause and take out the basket to flip the steak, and cover it with foil on top, for the remaining 14 minutes.
4. Once done, serve the medium-rare steak and enjoy it by resting for 10 minutes.
5. Serve by cutting in slices.
6. Enjoy.

Serving Suggestion: Serve it with mashed potatoes.

Variation Tip: Use vegetable oil instead of canola oil.

Nutritional Information Per Serving:

Calories 935| Fat 37.2g| Sodium 1419mg | Carbs 0g | Fiber 0g| Sugar 0g | Protein137.5 g

Beef Ribs I

Prep time: 10 minutes| **Cook time:** 18 minutes| **Serves:** 2

Ingredients

- 4 tablespoons barbecue spice rub
- 1 tablespoon kosher salt and black pepper
- 3 tablespoons brown sugar
- 2 pounds beef ribs (3-3 ½ pounds), cut in thirds
- 1 cup barbecue sauce

Directions

1. In a small bowl, add salt, pepper, brown sugar, and BBQ spice rub.
2. Grease the ribs with oil spray from both sides and then rub it with a spice mixture.
3. Adjust the ribs inside the Ninja Air Fryer, and set it to AIR FRY mode at 375 degrees F for 18 minutes.
4. Hit START/PAUSE and let the air fryer cook the ribs.
5. Once done, serve with the coating BBQ sauce.

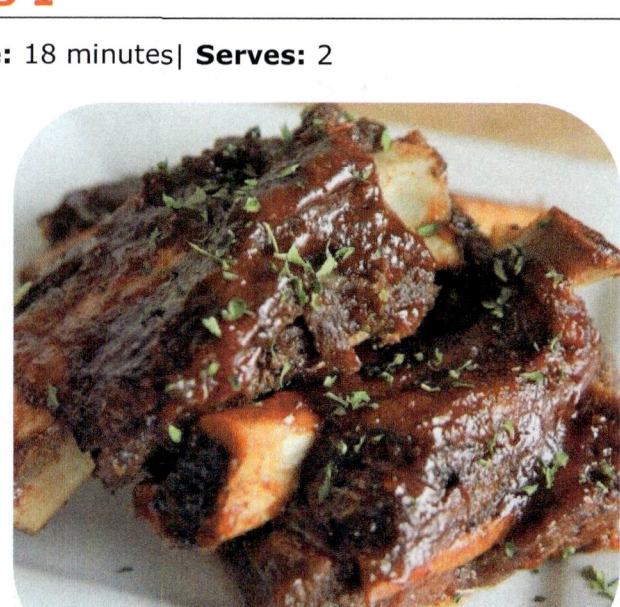

Serving Suggestion: Serve it with salad and baked potato.

Variation Tip: Use sea salt instead of kosher salt.

Nutritional Information Per Serving:

Calories1081 | Fat 28.6 g| Sodium 1701mg | Carbs 58g | Fiber 0.8g| Sugar 45.7g | Protein 138 g

Beef Ribs II

Prep time: 20 minutes| **Cook time:** 1 hour| **Serves:** 2

Ingredients for Marinade

- ¼ cup olive oil
- 4 garlic cloves, minced
- ½ cup white wine vinegar
- ¼ cup soy sauce, reduced-sodium
- ¼ cup Worcestershire sauce
- 1 lemon juice
- Salt and black pepper, to taste
- 2 tablespoons Italian seasoning
- 1 teaspoon smoked paprika
- 2 tablespoons mustard
- ½ cup maple syrup

Meat Ingredients

- Oil spray, for greasing
- 8 beef ribs lean

Directions

1. Preheat the unit by selecting AIR FRY mode for 2 minutes at 325 degrees F.
2. Select START/PAUSE to begin the preheating process.
3. Once preheating is done, press START/PAUSE.
1. Take a large bowl and add all the ingredients under marinade ingredients.
2. Put the marinade in a zip lock bag and add ribs to it.
3. Let it sit for 4 hours.
4. Now take out the basket of air fryer and grease the basket with oil spray.
5. Now put the ribs in the basket.
6. Set it to AIR FRY mode at 220 degrees F for 30 minutes.
7. Select Pause and take out the basket.
8. Afterward, flip the ribs and cook for 30 more minutes at 250 degrees F.
9. Once done, serve the juicy and tender ribs.
10. Enjoy.

Serving Suggestion: Serve it with Mac and cheese.

Variation Tip: Use garlic-infused oil instead of garlic cloves.

Nutritional Information Per Serving:

Calories 1927| Fat116g| Sodium 1394mg | Carbs 35.2g | Fiber 1.3g| Sugar29 g | Protein 172.3g

Chicken and Poultry Recipes

Crusted Chicken Breast

Prep time: 15 minutes| **Cook time:** 28 minutes| **Serves:** 4

Ingredients:

- 2 large eggs, beaten
- ½ cup all-purpose flour
- 1 ¼ cups panko bread crumbs
- ⅔ cup Parmesan, grated
- 4 teaspoons lemon zest
- 2 teaspoons dried oregano
- Salt, to taste
- 1 teaspoon cayenne pepper
- Freshly black pepper, to taste
- 4 boneless skinless chicken breasts

Preparation:

1. At 390 degrees F, preheat your Air Fryer on Air Fry mode.
2. Beat eggs in one shallow bowl and spread flour in another shallow bowl.
3. Mix panko with oregano, lemon zest, Parmesan, cayenne, oregano, salt, and black pepper in another shallow bowl.
4. First, coat the chicken with flour first, then dip it in the eggs and coat them with panko mixture.
5. Arrange the prepared chicken in the Air Fryer Basket.
6. Return the Air Fryer Basket to the Air Fryer and cook for 28 minutes.
7. Initiate cooking by pressing the START/PAUSE BUTTON.
8. Flip the half-cooked chicken and continue cooking until golden.
9. Serve warm.

Serving Suggestion: Serve with fresh-cut tomatoes and sautéed greens.

Variation Tip: Rub the chicken with lemon juice before seasoning.

Nutritional Information Per Serving:
Calories 220 | Fat 13g |Sodium 542mg | Carbs 0.9g | Fiber 0.3g | Sugar 0.2g | Protein 25.6g

Balsamic Duck Breast

Prep time: 15 minutes| **Cook time:** 20 minutes| **Serves:** 2

Ingredients:
- 2 Duck Breasts
- 1 teaspoon parsley
- Salt and black pepper, to taste

Marinade:
- 1 tablespoon olive oil
- ½ teaspoon French mustard
- 1 teaspoon dried garlic
- 2 teaspoons honey
- ½ teaspoon balsamic vinegar

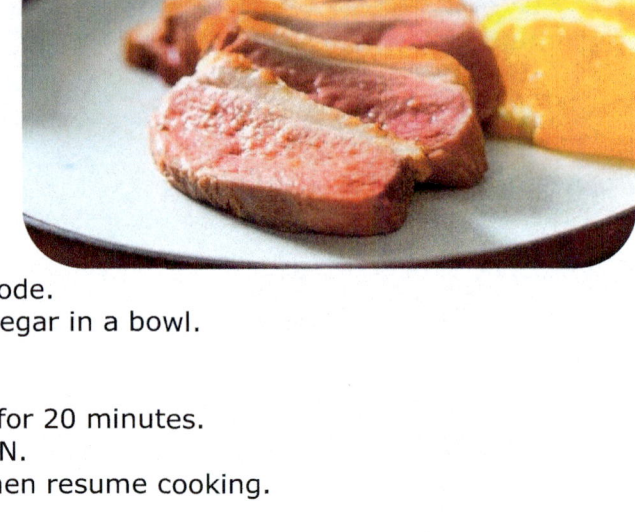

Preparation:
1. At 360 degrees F, preheat your Air Fryer on Air Fry mode.
2. Mix olive oil, mustard, garlic, honey, and balsamic vinegar in a bowl.
3. Add duck breasts to the marinade and rub well.
4. Place one duck breast in the Air Fryer Basket.
5. Return the Air Fryer Basket to the Air Fryer and cook for 20 minutes.
6. Initiate cooking by pressing the START/PAUSE BUTTON.
7. Flip the duck breasts once cooked halfway through, then resume cooking.
8. Serve warm.

Serving Suggestion: Serve with white rice and avocado salad

Variation Tip: Rub the duck breast with garlic cloves before seasoning.

Nutritional Information Per Serving:
Calories 546 | Fat 33.1g |Sodium 1201mg | Carbs 30g | Fiber 2.4g | Sugar 9.7g | Protein 32g

Chicken Wings

Prep time: 15 minutes| **Cook time:** 20 minutes| **Serves:** 3

Ingredients
- 1 cup chicken batter mix, Louisiana
- 9 Chicken wings
- ½ teaspoon smoked paprika
- 2 tablespoons Dijon mustard
- 1 tablespoon cayenne pepper
- 1 teaspoon meat tenderizer, powder
- Oil spray, for greasing

Directions
1. Pat dry chicken wings, and add mustard, paprika, meat tenderizer, and cayenne pepper.
2. Dredge it in the chicken batter mix.
3. Oil sprays the chicken wings.
4. Grease the basket of the air fryer.
5. Put the wings into the air fryer.
6. Set it to AIR FRY mode at 400 degrees F for 20 minutes
7. Hit START/PAUSE to begin with the cooking.
8. Once the cooking cycle complete, serve, and enjoy hot.

Serving Suggestion: Serve it with salad.

Variation Tip: Use American yellow mustard instead of Dijon mustard.

Nutritional Information Per Serving:
Calories621 | Fat 32.6g| Sodium 2016mg | Carbs 46.6g | Fiber 1.1g | Sugar 0.2g | Protein 32.1g

Pickled Chicken Fillets

Prep time: 15 minutes| **Cook time:** 28 minutes| **Serves:** 4

Ingredients:

- 2 boneless chicken breasts
- ½ cup dill pickle juice
- 2 eggs
- ½ cup milk
- 1 cup flour, all-purpose
- 2 tablespoons powdered sugar
- 2 tablespoons potato starch
- 1 teaspoon paprika
- 1 teaspoon of sea salt
- ½ teaspoon black pepper
- ½ teaspoon garlic powder
- ¼ teaspoon ground celery seed ground
- 1 tablespoon olive oil
- Cooking spray
- 4 hamburger buns, toasted
- 8 dill pickle chips

Preparation:

1. At 390 degrees F, preheat your Air Fryer on Air Fry mode.
2. Set the chicken in a suitable Ziplock bag and pound it into ½ thickness with a mallet.
3. Slice the chicken into 2 halves.
4. Add pickle juice and seal the bag.
5. Refrigerate for 30 minutes approximately for marination. Whisk both eggs with milk in a shallow bowl.
6. Thoroughly mix flour with spices and flour in a separate bowl.
7. Dip each chicken slice in egg, then in the flour mixture.
8. Shake off the excess and set the chicken pieces in the Air Fryer Basket.
9. Spray the pieces with cooking oil.
10. Place the chicken pieces in the Air Fryer Basket in a single layer and spray the cooking oil.
11. Return the Air Fryer Basket to the Air Fryer and cook for 28 minutes.
12. Initiate cooking by pressing the START/PAUSE BUTTON.
13. Flip the chicken pieces once cooked halfway through, and resume cooking.
14. Enjoy with pickle chips and a dollop of mayonnaise.

Serving Suggestion: Serve with warm corn tortilla and Greek salad.

Variation Tip: You can use the almond flour breading for a low-carb serving.

Nutritional Information Per Serving:

Calories 353 | Fat 5g |Sodium 818mg | Carbs 53.2g | Fiber 4.4g | Sugar 8g | Protein 17.3g

Chili Chicken Wings

Prep time: 20 minutes| **Cook time:** 43 minutes| **Serves:** 4

Ingredients:

- 8 chicken wings drumettes
- cooking spray
- ⅛ cup low-fat buttermilk
- ¼ cup almond flour
- McCormick chicken seasoning to taste

Thai Chili Marinade

- 1 ½ tablespoons low-sodium soy sauce
- ½ teaspoon ginger, minced
- 1 ½ garlic cloves
- 1 green onion
- ½ teaspoon rice wine vinegar
- ½ tablespoon Sriracha sauce
- ½ tablespoon sesame oil

Preparation:

1. At 390 degrees F, preheat your Air Fryer on Air Fry mode.
2. Put all the ingredients for the marinade in the blender and blend them for 1 minute.
3. Keep this marinade aside. Pat dry the washed chicken and place it in the Ziploc bag.
4. Add buttermilk, chicken seasoning, and zip the bag.
5. Shake the bag well, then refrigerator for 30 minutes for marination.
6. Remove the chicken drumettes from the marinade, then dredge them through dry flour.
7. Spread the drumettes in the Air Fryer Basket and spray them with cooking oil.
8. Return the Air Fryer Basket to the Air Fryer and cook for 43 minutes.
9. Initiate cooking by pressing the START/PAUSE BUTTON.
10. Toss the drumettes once cooked halfway through.
11. Now brush the chicken pieces with Thai chili sauce and then resume cooking.
12. Serve warm.

Serving Suggestion: Serve with warm corn tortilla and ketchup.

Variation Tip: Rub the wings with lemon or orange juice before cooking.

Nutritional Information Per Serving:

Calories 223 | Fat 11.7g |Sodium 721mg | Carbs 13.6g | Fiber 0.7g | Sugar 8g | Protein 15.7g

Air Fried Turkey Breast

Prep time: 10 minutes| **Cook time:** 46 minutes| **Serves:** 4

Ingredients:

- 2 lbs. turkey breast, on the bone with skin
- ½ tablespoon olive oil
- 1 teaspoon salt
- ¼ tablespoon dry poultry seasoning

Preparation:

1. At 390 degrees F, preheat your Air Fryer on Air Fry mode.
2. Rub turkey breast with ½ tablespoon of oil.
3. Season both its sides with turkey seasoning and salt, then rub in the brush half tablespoon of oil over the skin of the turkey.
4. Place the turkey in the Air Fryer Basket.
5. Return the Air Fryer Basket to the Air Fryer and cook for 46 minutes.
6. Initiate cooking by pressing the START/PAUSE BUTTON.
7. Flip the turkey once cooked halfway through, and resume cooking.
8. Slice and serve warm.

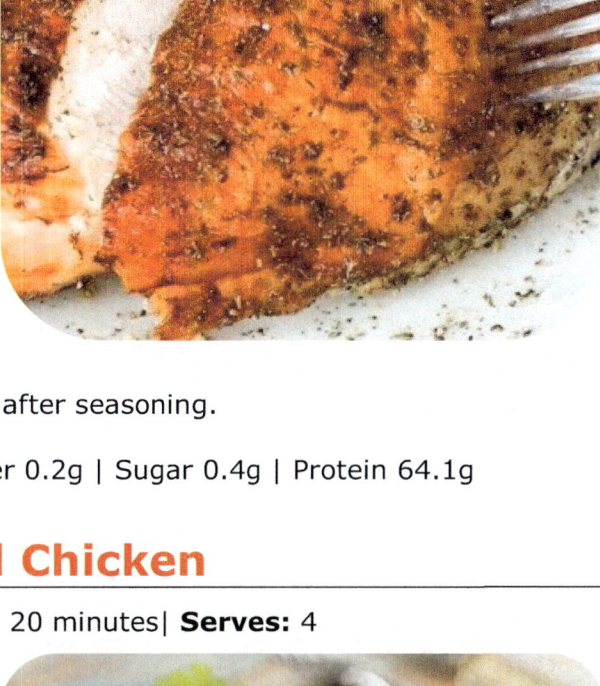

Serving Suggestion: Serve with warm corn tortilla and Greek salad.
Variation Tip: Coat and dust the turkey breast with flour after seasoning.
Nutritional Information Per Serving:
Calories 502 | Fat 25g |Sodium 230mg | Carbs 1.5g | Fiber 0.2g | Sugar 0.4g | Protein 64.1g

Cheddar-Stuffed Chicken

Prep time: 10 minutes| **Cook time:** 20 minutes| **Serves:** 4

Ingredients:

- 3 bacon strips, cooked and crumbled
- 2 ounces Cheddar cheese, cubed
- ¼ cup barbeque sauce
- 2 (4 ounces) boneless chicken breasts
- Salt and black pepper to taste

Preparation:

1. At 360 degrees F, preheat your Air Fryer on Air Fry mode.
2. Make a 1-inch deep pouch in each chicken breast.
3. Mix cheddar cubes with half of the BBQ sauce, salt, black pepper, and bacon.
4. Divide this filling in the chicken breasts and secure the edges with a toothpick.
5. Brush the remaining BBQ sauce over the chicken breasts.
6. Place the chicken in the Air Fryer Basket and spray them with cooking oil.
7. Return the Air Fryer Basket to the Air Fryer and cook for 20 minutes.
8. Initiate cooking by pressing the START/PAUSE BUTTON.
9. Serve warm.

Serving Suggestion: Serve with tomato salsa on top.
Variation Tip: Use poultry seasoning for breading.
Nutritional Information Per Serving:
Calories 379 | Fat 19g |Sodium 184mg | Carbs 12.3g | Fiber 0.6g | Sugar 2g | Protein 37.7g

Brazilian Chicken Drumsticks

Prep time: 15 minutes | **Cook time:** 27 minutes | **Serves:** 6

Ingredients:

- 2 teaspoons cumin seeds
- 2 teaspoons dried parsley
- 2 teaspoons turmeric powder
- 2 teaspoons dried oregano leaves
- 2 teaspoons salt
- 1 teaspoon coriander seeds
- 1 teaspoon black peppercorns
- 1 teaspoon cayenne pepper
- ½ cup lime juice
- 4 tablespoons vegetable oil
- 3 lbs. chicken drumsticks

Preparation:

1. At 390 degrees F, preheat your Air Fryer on Air Fry mode.
2. Grind cumin, parsley, salt, coriander seeds, cayenne pepper, peppercorns, oregano, and turmeric in a food processor.
3. Add this mixture to lemon juice and oil in a bowl and mix well.
4. Rub the spice paste over the chicken drumsticks and let them marinate for 30 minutes.
5. Place the chicken drumsticks in the Air Fryer Basket.
6. Return the Air Fryer Basket to the Air Fryer and cook for 27 minutes.
7. Initiate cooking by pressing the START/PAUSE BUTTON.
8. Flip the drumsticks when cooked halfway through, then resume cooking.
9. Serve warm.

Serving Suggestion: Serve with tomato ketchup or chili sauce.

Variation Tip: Use buttermilk to soak the drumsticks before seasoning.

Nutritional Information Per Serving:

Calories 456 | Fat 16.4g | Sodium 1321mg | Carbs 19.2g | Fiber 2.2g | Sugar 4.2g | Protein 55.2g

Veggie Stuffed Chicken Breasts

Prep time: 15 minutes | **Cook time:** 10 minutes | **Serves:** 2

Ingredients:

- 4 teaspoons chili powder
- 4 teaspoons ground cumin
- 1 skinless, boneless chicken breast
- 2 teaspoons chipotle flakes
- 2 teaspoons Mexican oregano
- Salt and black pepper, to taste
- ½ red bell pepper, julienned
- ½ onion, julienned
- 1 fresh jalapeno pepper, julienned
- 2 teaspoons corn oil
- ½ lime, juiced

Preparation:

1. At 360 degrees F, preheat your Air Fryer on Air Fry mode.
2. Slice the chicken breast in half horizontally.
3. Pound each chicken breast with a mallet into ¼-inch thickness.
4. Rub the pounded chicken breast with black pepper, salt, oregano, chipotle flakes, cumin, and chili powder.
5. Add ½ of bell pepper, jalapeno, and onion on top of each chicken breast piece.
6. Roll the chicken to wrap the filling inside and insert toothpicks to seal.
7. Place the rolls in the Air Fryer Basket and spray them with cooking oil.
8. Return the Air Fryer Basket to the Air Fryer and cook for 10 minutes.
9. Initiate cooking by pressing the START/PAUSE BUTTON.
10. Serve warm.

Serving Suggestion: Serve with tomato ketchup or chili sauce.

Variation Tip: Season the chicken rolls with seasoned parmesan before cooking.

Nutritional Information Per Serving:

Calories 351 | Fat 11g | Sodium 150mg | Carbs 3.3g | Fiber 0.2g | Sugar 1g | Protein 33.2g

Sweet and Spicy Carrots with Chicken Thighs

Prep time: 15 minutes| **Cook time:** 25 minutes| **Serves:** 2

Ingredients

Ingredients for Glaze

- Cooking spray, for greasing
- 2 tablespoons butter, melted
- 1 tablespoon hot honey
- 1 teaspoon orange zest
- 1 teaspoon cardamom
- ½ pound baby carrots
- 1 tablespoon orange juice
- Salt and black pepper, to taste

Other Ingredients

- ½ pound carrots, baby carrots
- 8 chicken thighs

Directions

1. Take a bowl and mix all the glaze ingredients in it.
2. Now, coat the chicken and carrots with the glaze and let it rest for 30 minutes.
3. Now place the chicken thighs and carrots into the air fryer basket.
4. Press start and set it to ROAST mode at 390 degrees F for 25 minutes.
5. After 12 minutes, take out the carrots and let the cooking cycle completes for chicken.
6. Then serve it hot.

Serving Suggestion: Serve with Salad.

Variation Tip: Use lime juice instead of orange juice.

Nutritional Information Per Serving:

Calories 1312| Fat 55.4g| Sodium 757mg | Carbs 23.3g | Fiber6.7 g | Sugar12 g | Protein171 g

Chicken Leg Piece

Prep time: 15 minutes| **Cook time:** 25 minutes| **Serves:** 1

Ingredients
- 1 teaspoon onion powder
- 1 teaspoon paprika powder
- 1 teaspoon garlic powder
- Salt and black pepper, to taste
- 1 tablespoon Italian seasoning
- 1 teaspoon celery seeds
- 2 eggs, whisked
- ⅓ cup buttermilk
- 1 cup corn flour
- 1 pound chicken leg

Directions
1. Take a bowl and whisk egg along with pepper, salt, and buttermilk.
2. Set it aside for further use.
3. Mix all the spices in a small separate bowl.
4. Dredge the chicken in egg wash then dredge it in seasoning.
5. Coat the chicken legs with oil spray.
6. At the end dust it with the corn flour.
7. Put the leg pieces into air fryer basket.
8. Set it to 400 degrees F, for 25 minutes.
9. Let the air fryer do the magic.
10. Once it's done, serve and enjoy.

Serving Suggestion: Serve it with cooked rice.
Variation Tip: Use water instead of buttermilk.
Nutritional Information Per Serving:
Calories 1511| Fat 52.3g| Sodium615 mg | Carbs 100g | Fiber 9.2g | Sugar 8.1g | Protein 154.2g

Yummy Chicken Breasts

Prep time: 15 minutes| **Cook time:** 25 minutes| **Serves:** 2

Ingredients
- 4 large chicken breasts, 6 ounces each
- 2 tablespoons oil bay seasoning
- 1 tablespoon Montreal chicken seasoning
- 1 teaspoon thyme
- ½ teaspoon paprika
- Salt, to taste
- oil spray, for greasing

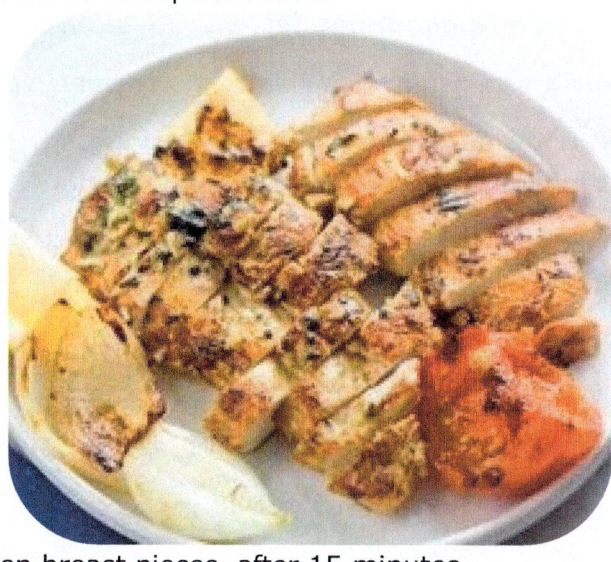

Directions
1. Season the chicken breast pieces with the listed seasoning and let them rest for 40 minutes.
2. Grease both sides of the chicken breast pieces with oil spray.
3. Put the chicken breast pieces inside the basket.
4. Set the AIR FRY mode at 400 degrees F, for 15 minutes.
5. Select pause and take out the basket and flip the chicken breast pieces, after 15 minutes.
6. Select AIR FRY at 400 degrees F, for 10 more minutes.
7. Once it's done serve.

Serving Suggestion: Serve it with baked potato.
Variation Tip: None
Nutritional Information Per Serving:
Calories 711| Fat 27.7g| Sodium 895mg | Carbs 1.6g | Fiber 0.4g | Sugar 0.1g | Protein 106.3g

Spiced Chicken and Vegetables

Prep time: 22 minutes| **Cook time:** 35 minutes| **Serves:** 1

Ingredients

- 2 large chicken breasts
- 2 teaspoons olive oil
- 1 teaspoon chili powder
- 1 teaspoon paprika powder
- 1 teaspoon onion powder
- ½ teaspoon garlic powder
- ¼ teaspoon Cumin
- Salt and black pepper, to taste

Vegetable Ingredients

- 2 large potato, cubed
- 4 large carrots cut into bite-size pieces
- 1 tablespoon olive oil
- Salt and black pepper, to taste

Directions

1. Take chicken breast pieces and rub olive oil, salt, pepper, chili powder, onion powder, cumin, garlic powder, and paprika.
2. Season the vegetables with olive oil, salt, and black pepper.
3. Now put the chicken breast pieces along with vegetables inside the air fryer basket.
4. Now set it to AIR FRY mode at 390 degrees F, for 35 minutes.
5. Once the cooking cycle is done, serve, and enjoy.

Serving Suggestion: Serve it with salad or ranch dressing.

Variation Tip: Use Canola oil instead of olive oil.

Nutritional Information Per Serving:

Calories1510 | Fat 51.3g| Sodium 525mg | Carbs 163g | Fiber24.7 g | Sugar 21.4g | Protein 102.9

Chicken Breast Strips

Prep time: 10 minutes| **Cook time:** 22 minutes| **Serves:** 2

Ingredient

- 2 large organic egg
- 1-ounce buttermilk
- 1 cup cornmeal
- ¼ cup all-purpose flour
- Salt and black pepper, to taste
- 1 pound chicken breasts, cut into strips
- 2 tablespoons oil bay seasoning
- oil spray, for greasing

Directions

1. Take a medium bowl and whisk eggs with buttermilk.
2. In a separate large bowl, mix flour, cornmeal, salt, black pepper, and oil bay seasoning.
3. First, dip the chicken breast strip in egg wash and then dredge into the flour mixture.
4. Coat the strip all over and layer it inside the basket that is already grease with oil spray.
5. Grease the chicken breast strips with oil spray as well.
6. Set the basket to AIR FRY mode at 400 degrees F for 22 minutes.
7. Hit the START/PAUSE button to let the cooking start.
8. Once the cooking cycle is done, serve.

Serving Suggestion: Serve it with roasted vegetables.

Variation Tip: None

Nutritional Information Per Serving:

Calories 788| Fat25g| Sodium835 mg | Carbs60g | Fiber 4.9g| Sugar1.5g | Protein79g

Cornish Hen with Asparagus

Prep time: 20 minutes | **Cook time:** 45 minutes | **Serves:** 2

Ingredients

- 10 spears asparagus
- Salt and black pepper, to taste
- 1 Cornish hen
- Salt, to taste
- Black pepper, to taste
- 1 teaspoon Paprika
- Coconut spray, for greasing
- 2 lemons, sliced

Directions

1. Wash and pat dry the asparagus and coat it with coconut oil spray.
2. Sprinkle salt on the asparagus and place inside the bottom of the basket of the air fryer.
3. Next, take the Cornish hen and rub it well with the salt, black pepper, and paprika.
4. Oil sprays the Cornish hen and place it on top of asparagus inside the air fryer basket.
5. Set the time to 45 minutes at 350 degrees F, by selecting the ROAST mode.
6. Once the 6 minutes pass hit START/PAUSE button and take out the asparagus.
7. Put the basket back in unit.
8. Once the chicken cooking cycle complete, transfer chicken to the serving plate.
9. Serve the chicken with roasted asparagus and slices of lemon.
10. Serve hot and enjoy.

Serving Suggestion: Serve it with ranch dressing.

Variation Tip: You can add variation by choosing chopped cilantro instead of a lemon slice.

Nutritional Information Per Serving:

Calories 192 | Fat 4.7g | Sodium 151mg | Carbs 10.7 g | Fiber 4.6g | Sugar 3.8g | Protein 30g

Seafood and Fish Recipes

Salmon Patties

Prep time: 15 minutes| **Cook time:** 18 minutes| **Serves:** 8

Ingredients:

- 1 lb. fresh Atlantic salmon side
- ¼ cup avocado, mashed
- ¼ cup cilantro, diced
- 1 ½ teaspoons yellow curry powder
- ½ teaspoons sea salt
- ¼ cup, 4 teaspoons tapioca starch
- 2 brown eggs
- ½ cup coconut flakes
- Coconut oil, melted, for brushing

For the greens:

- 2 teaspoons organic coconut oil, melted
- 6 cups arugula & spinach mix, tightly packed
- Pinch of sea salt

Preparation:

1. At 390 degrees F, preheat your Air Fryer on Air Fry mode.
2. Remove the fish skin and dice the flesh.
3. Place in a large bowl. Add cilantro, avocado, salt, and curry powder mix gently.
4. Add tapioca starch and mix well again.
5. Make 8 salmon patties out of this mixture, about a half-inch thick.
6. Place them on a baking sheet lined with wax paper and freeze them for 20 minutes.
7. Place ¼ cup of tapioca starch and coconut flakes on a flat plate.
8. Dip the patties in the whisked egg, then coat the frozen patties in the starch and flakes.
9. Place the patties in the Air Fryer Basket and spray them with cooking oil.
10. Return the Air Fryer Basket to the Air Fryer and cook for 17 minutes.
11. Initiate cooking by pressing the START/PAUSE BUTTON.
12. Flip the patties once cooked halfway through, then resume cooking.
13. Sauté arugula with spinach in coconut oil in a pan for 30 seconds.
14. Serve the patties with sautéed greens mixture.

Serving Suggestion: Serve with sautéed green beans or asparagus.

Variation Tip: Add lemon juice to the mixture before mixing.

Nutritional Information Per Serving:

Calories 260 | Fat 16g |Sodium 585mg | Carbs 3.1g | Fiber 1.3g | Sugar 0.2g | Protein 25.5g

Salmon Nuggets

Prep time: 15 minutes| **Cook time:** 15 minutes| **Serves:** 4

Ingredients:

- ⅓ cup maple syrup
- ¼ teaspoon dried chipotle pepper
- 1 pinch sea salt
- 1 ½ cups croutons
- 1 large egg
- 1 (1 pound) skinless salmon fillet, cut into 1 ½-inch chunk
- cooking spray

Preparation:

1. At 390 degrees F, preheat your Air Fryer on Air Fry mode.
2. Mix chipotle powder, maple syrup, and salt in a saucepan and cook on a simmer for 5 minutes.
3. Crush the croutons in a food processor and transfer them to a bowl.
4. Beat egg in another shallow bowl.
5. Season the salmon chunks with sea salt.
6. Dip the salmon in the egg, then coat with breadcrumbs.
7. Spread the coated salmon chunks in the Air Fryer Basket.
8. Return the Air Fryer Basket to the Air Fryer and cook for 10 minutes.
9. Initiate cooking by pressing the START/PAUSE BUTTON.
10. Flip the chunks once cooked halfway through, then resume cooking.
11. Pour the maple syrup on top and serve warm.

Serving Suggestion: Serve with creamy dip and crispy fries.

Variation Tip: Use crushed cornflakes for breading to have extra crispiness.

Nutritional Information Per Serving:
Calories 275 | Fat 1.4g |Sodium 582mg | Carbs 31.5g | Fiber 1.1g | Sugar 0.1g | Protein 29.8g

Breaded Scallops

Prep time: 15 minutes| **Cook time:** 12 minutes| **Serves:** 4

Ingredients:

- ½ cup crushed buttery crackers
- ½ teaspoon garlic powder
- ½ teaspoon seafood seasoning
- 2 tablespoons butter, melted
- 1-pound sea scallops patted dry
- cooking spray

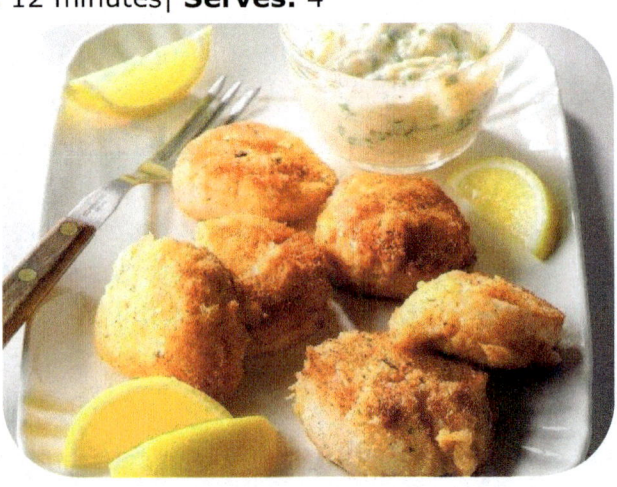

Preparation:

1. At 390 degrees F, preheat your Air Fryer on Air Fry mode.
2. Mix cracker crumbs, garlic powder, and seafood seasoning in a shallow bowl. Spread melted butter in another shallow bowl.
3. Dip each scallop in the melted butter and then roll in the breading to coat well.
4. Grease the Air Fryer Basket with cooking spray and place the scallops inside.
5. Return the Air Fryer Basket to the Air Fryer and cook for 12 minutes.
6. Initiate cooking by pressing the START/PAUSE BUTTON.
7. Flip the scallops with a spatula after 4 minutes and resume cooking.
8. Serve warm.

Serving Suggestion: Serve with creamy dip and crispy fries.

Variation Tip: Use crushed cornflakes for breading to have extra crispiness.

Nutritional Information Per Serving:
Calories 275 | Fat 1.4g |Sodium 582mg | Carbs 31.5g | Fiber 1.1g | Sugar 0.1g | Protein 29.8g

Fried Lobster Tails

Prep time: 10 minutes| **Cook time:** 18 minutes| **Serves:** 4

Ingredients:

- 4 (4 oz) lobster tails
- 8 tablespoons butter, melted
- 2 teaspoons lemon zest
- 2 garlic cloves, grated
- Salt and black pepper ground to taste
- 2 teaspoons fresh parsley, chopped
- 4 wedges lemon

Preparation:

1. At 350 degrees F, preheat your Air Fryer on Air Fry mode.
2. Spread the lobster tails into butterfly, slit the top to expose the lobster meat while keeping the tail intact.
3. Place the lobster tails in the Air Fryer Basket with their lobster meat facing up.
4. Mix melted butter with lemon zest and garlic in a bowl.
5. Brush the butter mixture on top of the lobster tails.
6. And drizzle salt and black pepper on top.
7. Return the Air Fryer Basket to the Air Fryer and cook for 18 minutes.
8. Initiate cooking by pressing the START/PAUSE BUTTON.
9. Garnish with parsley and lemon wedges.
10. Serve warm.

Serving Suggestion: Serve on a bed of lettuce leaves.

Variation Tip: Drizzle crushed cornflakes on top to have extra crispiness.

Nutritional Information Per Serving:

Calories 257 | Fat 10.4g |Sodium 431mg | Carbs 20g | Fiber 0g | Sugar 1.6g | Protein 21g

Scallops with Greens

Prep time: 15 minutes| **Cook time:** 13 minutes| **Serves:** 8

Ingredients:

- ¾ cup heavy whipping cream
- 1 tablespoon tomato paste
- 1 tablespoon chopped fresh basil
- 1 teaspoon garlic, minced
- ½ teaspoon salt
- ½ teaspoon pepper
- 12 ounces frozen spinach thawed
- 8 jumbo sea scallops
- Vegetable oil to spray

Preparation:

1. At 390 degrees F, preheat your Air Fryer on Air Fry mode.
2. Season the scallops with vegetable oil, salt, and pepper in a bowl.
3. Mix cream with spinach, basil, garlic, salt, pepper, and tomato paste in a bowl.
4. Pour this mixture over the scallops and mix gently.
5. Place the scallops in the Air Fryers Basket without using the crisper plate.
6. Return the Air Fryer Basket to the Air Fryer and cook for 13 minutes.
7. Initiate cooking by pressing the START/PAUSE BUTTON.
8. Serve right away.

Serving Suggestion: Serve with fresh cucumber salad.

Variation Tip: Use crushed cornflakes for breading to have extra crispiness.

Nutritional Information Per Serving:

Calories 266 | Fat 6.3g |Sodium 193mg | Carbs 39.1g | Fiber 7.2g | Sugar 5.2g | Protein 14.8g

Salmon with Fennel Salad

Prep time: 10 minutes| **Cook time:** 17 minutes| **Serves:** 4

Ingredients:
- 2 teaspoons fresh parsley, chopped
- 1 teaspoon fresh thyme, chopped
- 1 teaspoon salt
- 4 (6-oz) skinless center-cut salmon fillets
- 2 tablespoons olive oil
- 4 cups fennel, sliced
- ⅔ cup Greek yogurt
- 1 garlic clove, grated
- 2 tablespoons orange juice
- 1 teaspoon lemon juice
- 2 tablespoons fresh dill, chopped

Preparation:
1. At 390 degrees F, preheat your Air Fryer on Air Fry mode.
2. Mix ½ teaspoon of salt, thyme, and parsley in a small bowl.
3. Brush the salmon with oil first, then rub liberally rub the herb mixture.
4. Place salmon fillets in the Air Fryer Basket.
5. Return the Air Fryer Basket to the Air Fryer and cook for 17 minutes.
6. Initiate cooking by pressing the START/PAUSE BUTTON.
7. Meanwhile, mix fennel with garlic, yogurt, lemon juice, orange juice, remaining salt, and dill in a mixing bowl.
8. Serve the air fried salmon fillets with fennel salad.
9. Enjoy.

Serving Suggestion: Serve with melted butter on top.
Variation Tip: Rub the salmon with lemon juice before cooking.
Nutritional Information Per Serving:
Calories 305 | Fat 15g |Sodium 482mg | Carbs 17g | Fiber 3g | Sugar 2g | Protein 35g

Two-Way Salmon

Prep time: 10 minutes| **Cook time:** 18 minutes| **Serves:** 2

Ingredients
- 2 salmon fillets, 8 ounces each
- 2 tablespoons Cajun seasoning
- 2 tablespoons jerk seasoning
- 1 lemon cut in half
- Oil spray, for greasing

Directions
1. First, drizzle lemon juice over the salmon and wash it with tap water.
2. Rinse and pat dry the fillets with a paper towel.
3. Now rub o fillet with Cajun seasoning and grease it with oil spray.
4. Take the second fillet and rub it with jerk seasoning.
5. Grease the second fillet of salmon with oil spray.
6. Now put the salmon fillets in the air fryer basket.
7. Set the basket to 390 degrees F for 16-18 minutes at AIR FRY mode.
8. Hit the START/PAUSE button to start cooking.
9. Once the cooking is done, serve the fish fillets hot with mayonnaise.

Serving Suggestion: Serve it with ranch.
Variation Tip: None.
Nutritional Information Per Serving:
Calories 238| Fat 11.8g| Sodium 488mg | Carbs 9g | Fiber 0g | Sugar 8g | Protein 35g

Seafood Shrimp Omelet

Prep time: 20 minutes| **Cook time:** 15 minutes| **Serves:** 2

Ingredient

- 6 large shrimp, shells removed and chopped
- 6 eggs, beaten
- ½ tablespoon butter, melted
- 2 tablespoons green onions, sliced
- ⅓ cup mushrooms, chopped
- 1 pinch paprika
- Salt and black pepper, to taste
- Oil spray, for greasing

Directions

1. In a large bowl, whisk the eggs and add chopped shrimp, butter, green onions, mushrooms, paprika, salt, and black pepper.
2. Take a cake pan that fit inside the air fryer and grease them with oil spray.
3. Pour the egg mixture in the cake pan and place it inside the basket of the air fryer.
4. Turn on the Air Fry function, and let it cook for 15 minutes at 320 degrees F.
5. Once the cooking cycle completes, take out, and serve hot.

Serving Suggestion: Serve it with rice.

Variation Tip: Use olive oil for greasing purposes.

Nutritional Information Per Serving:

Calories 300 | Fat 17.5g| Sodium 368mg | Carbs 2.9g | Fiber 0.3g | Sugar1.4 g | Protein32.2 g

Salmon with Green Beans

Prep time: 12 minutes | **Cook time:** 18 minutes | **Serves:** 1

Ingredients

- 1 salmon fillet, 2 inches thick
- 2 teaspoons olive oil
- 2 teaspoons smoked paprika
- Salt and black pepper, to taste
- 1 cup green beans
- Oil spray, for greasing

Directions

1. Grease the green beans with oil spray and set aside for further use,
2. Now rub the salmon fillet with olive oil, smoked paprika, salt, and black pepper.
3. Put the salmon fillets in the basket of air fryer along with green beans.
4. You can adjust the green beans on a rack as well.
5. Now set it to AIR FRY mode at 350 degrees F for 18 minutes.
6. Once done, take out the salmon and green beans and transfer them to the serving plates and enjoy.

Serving Suggestion: Serve it with ranch dressing.

Variation Tip: Use any other green vegetable of your choice.

Nutritional Information Per Serving:
Calories 367| Fat 22g| Sodium 87mg | Carbs 10.2g | Fiber 5.3g | Sugar 2g | Protein 37.2g

Fish and Chips

Prep time: 15 minutes | **Cook time:** 22 minutes | **Serves:** 2

Ingredients

- 1 pound potatoes, cut lengthwise
- 1 cup seasoned flour
- 2 eggs, organic
- ⅓ cup buttermilk
- 2 cup seafood fry mix
- ½ cup bread crumbs
- 2 codfish fillet, 6 ounces each
- Oil spray, for greasing

Directions

1. Take a bowl and whisk eggs in it along buttermilk.
2. In a separate bowl, mix seafood fry mix and bread crumbs
3. Take a baking tray and spread flour on it.
4. Dip the fillets first in egg wash, then in flour, and at the end coat it with breadcrumbs mixture.
5. Put the fish fillet in air fryer basket.
6. Grease the fish fillet with oil spray.
7. Put potato chips inside the basket and lightly grease it with oil spray.
8. Set the air fryer to AIR FRY mode at 400 degrees F for 22 minutes.
9. After 12 minutes take out the fish and continue with the cooking cycle.
10. Once done, serve and enjoy.

Serving Suggestion: Serve it with mayonnaise.

Variation Tip: Use water instead of buttermilk.

Nutritional Information Per Serving:
Calories 992| Fat 22.3g| Sodium1406 mg | Carbs 153.6g | Fiber 10g | Sugar 10g | Protein 40g

Frozen Breaded Fish Fillet

Prep time: 15 minutes | **Cook time:** 12 minutes | **Serves:** 2

Ingredients

- 4 frozen breaded fish fillet
- Oil spray, for greasing
- 1 cup mayonnaise

Directions

1. Take the frozen fish fillets out of the bag and place them in the basket of the air fryer.
2. Lightly grease it with oil spray.
3. Set the unit to 380 degrees F for 12 minutes at AIR FRY mode.
4. Hit the START/PAUSE button to start cooking.
5. Once the cooking is done, serve the fish hot with mayonnaise.

Serving Suggestion: Serve it with salad and rice.

Variation Tip: Use olive oil instead of butter.

Nutritional Information per Serving:
Calories 921| Fat 61.5g| Sodium 1575mg | Carbs 69g | Fiber 2g | Sugar 9.5g | Protein 29.1g

Keto Baked Salmon with Pesto

Prep time: 15 minutes| **Cook time:** 18 minutes| **Serves:** 2

Ingredients
- 4 salmon fillets, 2 inches thick
- 2 ounces green pesto
- Salt and black pepper
- ½ tablespoon canola oil, for greasing

Ingredients for Green Sauce
- 1-½ cup mayonnaise
- 2 tablespoons Greek yogurt
- Salt and black pepper, to taste

Directions
1. Rub the salmon with pesto, salt, oil, and black pepper.
2. In a small bowl, whisk together all the green sauce ingredients.
3. Put the fish fillets in the basket.
4. Set the AIR FRY mode for 18 minutes at 390 degrees F.
5. Once the cooking is done, serve it with green sauce drizzle.
6. Enjoy.

Serving Suggestion: Serve it with mashed cheesy potatoes.
Variation Tip: Use butter instead of canal oil.
Nutritional Information Per Serving:
Calories 1165 | Fat80.7 g| Sodium 1087 mg | Carbs 33.1g | Fiber 0.5g | Sugar11.5 g | Protein 80.6g

Crusted Tilapia

Prep time: 20 minutes| **Cook time:** 17 minutes| **Serves:** 4

Ingredients:
- ¾ cup breadcrumbs
- 1 packet dry ranch-style dressing
- 2 ½ tablespoons vegetable oil
- 2 eggs beaten
- 4 tilapia fillets
- Herbs and chilies to garnish

Preparation:
1. At 390 degrees F, preheat your Air Fryer on Air Fry mode.
2. Thoroughly mix ranch dressing with panko in a bowl.
3. Whisk eggs in a shallow bowl.
4. Dip each fish fillet in the egg, then coat evenly with the panko mixture.
5. Set two coated fillets in the Air Fryer Basket.
6. Return the Air Fryer Basket to the Air Fryer and cook for 17 minutes.
7. Initiate cooking by pressing the START/PAUSE BUTTON.
8. Serve warm with herbs and chilies

Serving Suggestion: Serve with sautéed asparagus on the side.
Variation Tip: Coat the fish with crushed cornflakes for extra crispiness.
Nutritional Information Per Serving:
Calories 196 | Fat 7.1g |Sodium 492mg | Carbs 21.6g | Fiber 2.9g | Sugar 0.8g | Protein 13.4g

Codfish with Herb Vinaigrette

Prep time: 15 minutes| **Cook time:** 16 minutes| **Serves:** 2

Ingredients

Vinaigrette Ingredients

- ½ cup parsley leaves
- 1 cup basil leaves
- ½ cup mint leaves
- 2 tablespoons thyme leaves
- ¼ teaspoon red pepper flakes
- 2 cloves garlic
- 4 tablespoons red wine vinegar
- ¼ cup olive oil
- Salt, to taste

Other Ingredients

- 1.5 pounds fish fillets, cod fish
- 2 tablespoons olive oil
- Salt and black pepper, to taste
- 1 teaspoon paprika
- 1 teaspoon Italian seasoning

Directions

1. Blend the entire vinaigrette ingredient in a high-speed blender and pulse into a smooth paste.
2. Set aside for drizzling overcooked fish.
3. Rub the fillets with salt, black pepper, paprika, Italian seasoning, and olive oil.

Put it to the basket of the air fryer.

4. Set it to 16 minutes at 390 degrees F, on AIR FRY mode.
5. Once done, serve the fillets with the drizzle of blended vinaigrette.

Serving Suggestion: Serve it with rice.

Variation Tip: Use sour cream instead of cream cheese.

Nutritional Information Per Serving:

Calories 1219| Fat 81.8g| Sodium 1906mg | Carbs 64.4g | Fiber 5.5g | Sugar 0.4g | Protein 52.1g

Lemon Pepper Salmon with Asparagus

Prep time: 20 minutes| **Cook time:** 20 minutes| **Serves:** 2

Ingredients

- 1 cup green asparagus
- 2 tablespoons butter
- 2 fillets salmon, 8 ounces each
- Salt and black pepper, to taste
- 1 teaspoon lemon juice
- ½ teaspoon lemon zest
- oil spray, for greasing

Directions

1. Rinse and trim the asparagus.
2. Rinse and pat dry the salmon fillets.
3. Take a bowl and mix lemon juice, lemon zest, salt, and black pepper.
4. Brush the fish fillet with the rub and place it in the basket along with asparagus.
5. Set it to AIR FRY mode for 20 minutes at 390 degrees F.
6. Once 5 minutes passes, take out the basket and remove asparagus.
7. Continue with the cooking cycle.
8. Once done, serve and enjoy.

Serving Suggestion: Serve it with baked potato.

Variation Tip: Use olive oil instead of butter.

Nutritional Information Per Serving:

Calories 482| Fat 28g| Sodium209 mg | Carbs 2.8g | Fiber1.5 g | Sugar1.4 g | Protein 56.3g

Vegetables Recipes

Garlic Potato Wedges in Air Fryer

Prep time: 10 minutes| **Cook time:** 20 minutes| **Serves:** 2

Ingredients

- 4 medium potatoes, peeled and cut into wedges
- 4 tablespoons butter
- 1 teaspoon chopped cilantro
- 1 cup plain flour
- 1 teaspoon garlic, minced
- Salt and black pepper, to taste

Directions

1. Soak the potatoes wedges in cold water for about 30 minutes.
2. Then drain and pat dry with a paper towel.
3. Boil water in a large pot and boil the wedges just for 3 minutes.
4. Then take it out on a paper towel.
5. Now in bowl mix garlic, melted butter, salt, pepper, cilantro and whisk it well.
6. Add the flour to a separate bowl and add salt and black pepper.
7. Then add water to the flour so it gets runny in texture.
8. Now, coat the potatoes with flour mixture and add it to a foil tin.
9. Put foil tin in the air fryer basket.
10. Now, set time using AIR FRY mode at 390 degrees F for 20 minutes.
11. Once done, serve and enjoy.

Serving Suggestion: Serve with ketchup.

Variation Tip: Use olive oil instead of butter.

Nutritional Information Per Serving:

Calories 727| Fat 24.1g| Sodium 191mg | Carbs 115.1g | Fiber 12g | Sugar 5.1g | Protein14 g

Curly Fries

Prep time: 10 minutes| **Cook time:** 20 minutes| **Serves:** 6

Ingredients:

- 2 spiralized zucchinis
- 1 cup flour
- 2 tablespoons paprika
- 1 teaspoon cayenne pepper
- 1 teaspoon garlic powder
- 1 teaspoon black pepper
- 1 teaspoon salt
- 2 eggs
- olive oil or cooking spray

Preparation:

1. At 390 degrees F, preheat your Air Fryer on Air Fry mode.
2. Mix flour with paprika, cayenne pepper, garlic powder, black pepper, and salt in a bowl.
3. Beat eggs in another bowl and dip the zucchini in the eggs.
4. Coat the zucchini with the flour mixture and place into the Air Fryer Basket.
5. Spray the zucchini with cooking oil.
6. Return the Air Fryer Basket to the Air Fryer and cook for 20 minutes.
7. Initiate cooking by pressing the START/PAUSE BUTTON.
8. Toss the zucchini once cooked halfway through, then resume cooking.
9. Serve warm.

Serving Suggestion: Serve with red chunky salsa or chili sauce.

Variation Tip: Use crushed cornflakes for breading to have extra crispiness.

Nutritional Information Per Serving:

Calories 212 | Fat 11.8g |Sodium 321mg | Carbs 24.6g | Fiber 4.4g | Sugar 8g | Protein 7.3g

Fried Olives

Prep time: 15 minutes| **Cook time:** 9 minutes| **Serves:** 6

Ingredients:

- 2 cups blue cheese stuffed olives, drained
- ½ cup all-purpose flour
- 1 cup panko breadcrumbs
- ½ teaspoon garlic powder
- 1 pinch oregano
- 2 eggs

Preparation:

1. At 375 degrees F, preheat your Air Fryer on Air Fry mode.
2. Mix flour with oregano and garlic powder in a bowl and beat two eggs in another bowl.
3. Spread panko breadcrumbs in a bowl.
4. Coat all the olives with the flour mixture, dip in the eggs and then coat with the panko breadcrumbs.
5. As you coat the olives, place them in the Air Fryer Basket in a single layer, then spray them with cooking oil.
6. Return the Air Fryer Basket to the Air Fryer and cook for 9 minutes.
7. Initiate cooking by pressing the START/PAUSE BUTTON.
8. Flip the olives once cooked halfway through, then resume cooking.
9. Serve.

Serving Suggestion: Serve with red chunky salsa or chili sauce.

Variation Tip: Use crushed cornflakes for breading to have extra crispiness.

Nutritional Information Per Serving:

Calories 166 | Fat 3.2g |Sodium 437mg | Carbs 28.8g | Fiber 1.8g | Sugar 2.7g | Protein 5.8g

Quinoa Patties

Prep time: 15 minutes| **Cook time:** 32 minutes| **Serves:** 4

Ingredients:

- 1 cup quinoa red
- 1½ cups water
- 1 teaspoon salt
- black pepper, ground
- 1½ cups rolled oats
- 3 eggs beaten
- ¼ cup minced white onion
- ½ cup crumbled feta cheese
- ¼ cup chopped fresh chives
- Salt and black pepper, to taste
- Vegetable or canola oil
- 4 hamburger buns
- 4 arugulas
- 4 slices tomato sliced

Cucumber yogurt dill sauce
- 1 cup cucumber, diced

- 1 cup Greek yogurt
- 2 teaspoons lemon juice
- ¼ teaspoon salt
- Black pepper, ground
- 1 tablespoon chopped fresh dill
- 1 tablespoon olive oil

Preparation:

1. At 390 degrees F, preheat your Air Fryer on Air Fry mode.
2. Add quinoa to a saucepan filled with cold water, salt, and black pepper, and place it over medium-high heat.
3. Cook the quinoa to a boil, then reduce the heat, cover, and cook for 20 minutes on a simmer.
4. Fluff and mix the cooked quinoa with a fork and remove it from the heat.
5. Spread the quinoa in a baking stay.
6. Mix eggs, oats, onion, herbs, cheese, salt, and black pepper.
7. Stir in quinoa, then mix well. Make 4 patties out of this quinoa cheese mixture.
8. Place the patties in the Air Fryer Basket and spray them with cooking oil.
9. Return the Air Fryer Basket to the Air Fryer and cook for 13 minutes.
10. Initiate cooking by pressing the START/PAUSE BUTTON.
11. Flip the patties once cooked halfway through, and resume cooking.
12. Meanwhile, prepare the cucumber yogurt dill sauce by mixing all of its ingredients in a mixing bowl.
13. Place each quinoa patty in a burger bun along with arugula leaves.
14. Serve with yogurt dill sauce.

Serving Suggestion: Serve with yogurt dip.

Variation Tip: Use crushed cornflakes for breading to have extra crispiness.

Nutritional Information Per Serving:

Calories 231 | Fat 9g |Sodium 271mg | Carbs 32.8g | Fiber 6.4g | Sugar 7g | Protein 6.3g

Sweet Potatoes with Honey Butter

Prep time: 15 minutes| **Cook time:** 40 minutes| **Serves:** 4

Ingredients:

- 4 sweet potatoes, scrubbed
- 1 teaspoon oil

Honey Butter

- 4 tablespoons unsalted butter
- 1 tablespoon honey
- 2 teaspoons hot sauce
- ¼ teaspoon salt

Preparation:

1. At 390 degrees F, preheat your Air Fryer on Air Fry mode.
2. Rub the sweet potatoes with oil and place two potatoes in the Air Fryer Basket.
3. Return the Air Fryer Basket to the Air Fryer and cook for 40 minutes.
4. Initiate cooking by pressing the START/PAUSE BUTTON.
5. Flip the potatoes once cooked halfway through, then resume cooking.
6. Mix butter with hot sauce, honey, and salt in a bowl.
7. When the potatoes are done, cut a slit on top and make a well with a spoon.
8. Pour the honey butter into each potato jacket.
9. Serve.

Serving Suggestion: Serve with sautéed vegetables and salad.

Variation Tip: Sprinkle crumbled bacon and parsley on top.

Nutritional Information Per Serving:

Calories 288 | Fat 6.9g |Sodium 761mg | Carbs 46g | Fiber 4g | Sugar 12g | Protein 9.6g

Fried Artichoke Hearts

Prep time: 15 minutes| **Cook time:** 10 minutes| **Serves:** 6

Ingredients:

- 3 cans Quartered Artichokes, drained
- ½ cup mayonnaise
- 1 cup panko breadcrumbs
- ⅓ cup grated Parmesan
- salt and black pepper to taste
- Parsley for garnish

Preparation:

1. At 375 degrees F, preheat your Air Fryer on Air Fry mode.
2. Mix mayonnaise with salt and black pepper and keep the sauce aside.
3. Spread panko breadcrumbs in a bowl.
4. Coat the artichoke pieces with the breadcrumbs.
5. As you coat the artichokes, place them in the Air Fryer Basket in a single layer, then spray them with cooking oil.
6. Return the Air Fryer Basket to the Air Fryer and cook for 10 minutes.
7. Initiate cooking by pressing the START/PAUSE BUTTON.
8. Flip the artichokes once cooked halfway through, then resume cooking.
9. Serve warm with mayo sauce.

Serving Suggestion: Serve with red chunky salsa or chili sauce.

Variation Tip: Use crushed cornflakes for breading to have extra crispiness.

Nutritional Information Per Serving:

Calories 193 | Fat 1g |Sodium 395mg | Carbs 38.7g | Fiber 1.6g | Sugar 0.9g | Protein 6.6g

Zucchini Cakes

Prep time: 10 minutes| **Cook time:** 32 minutes| **Serves:** 6

Ingredients:
- 2 medium zucchinis, grated
- 1 cup corn kernel
- 1 medium potato cooked
- 2 tablespoons chickpea flour
- 2 garlic minced
- 2 teaspoons olive oil
- Salt and black pepper

For Serving:
- Yogurt tahini sauce

Preparation:
1. At 390 degrees F, preheat your Air Fryer on Air Fry mode.
2. Mix grated zucchini with a pinch of salt in a colander and leave them for 15 minutes.
3. Squeeze out their excess water.
4. Mash the cooked potato in a large-sized bowl with a fork.
5. Add zucchini, corn, garlic, chickpea flour, salt, and black pepper to the bowl.
6. Mix these fritters' ingredients together and make 2 tablespoons-sized balls out of this mixture and flatten them lightly.
7. Place the fritters in the Air Fryer Basket in a single layer and spray them with cooking.
8. Return the Air Fryer Basket to the Air Fryer and cook for 17 minutes.
9. Initiate cooking by pressing the START/PAUSE BUTTON.
10. Flip the fritters once cooked halfway through, then resume cooking.
11. Serve.

Serving Suggestion: Serve with mayonnaise or cream cheese dip.
Variation Tip: Use crushed cornflakes for breading to have extra crispiness.
Nutritional Information Per Serving:
Calories 270 | Fat 14.6g |Sodium 394mg | Carbs 31.3g | Fiber 7.5g | Sugar 9.7g | Protein 6.4g

Green Beans with Baked Potatoes

Prep time: 15 minutes| **Cook time:** 45 minutes| **Serves:** 2

Ingredients
- 2 cups green beans
- 2 large potatoes, cubed
- 3 tablespoons olive oil
- 1 teaspoon seasoned salt
- ½ teaspoon chili powder
- 1/6 teaspoon garlic powder
- ¼ teaspoon onion powder

Directions
1. Take a large bowl and pour olive oil into it.
2. Now add all the seasoning in the olive oil and whisk it well.
3. Toss the green bean in it, and then transfer it to the basket of the air fryer.
4. Now season the potatoes with the seasoning and add them to the basket as well.
5. Now set the unit to AIR FRY mode at 350 degrees F for 45 minutes.
6. After 18 minutes take out the asparagus and continue with cooking.
7. Once the cooking cycle is complete, take out and serve it by transferring it to the serving plates.

Serving Suggestion: Serve with rice.
Variation Tip: Use canola oil instead of olive oil.
Nutritional Information Per Serving:
Calories473 | Fat21.6g | Sodium796 mg | Carbs 66.6g | Fiber12.9 g | Sugar6 g | Protein8.4 g

Zucchini with Stuffing

Prep time: 12 minutes| **Cook time:** 20 minutes| **Serves:** 3

Ingredients

- 1 cup quinoa, rinsed
- 1 cup black olives
- 6 medium zucchinis, about 2 pounds
- 2 cups cannellini beans, drained
- 1 white onion, chopped
- ¼ cup almonds, chopped
- 4 cloves garlic, chopped
- 4 tablespoons olive oil
- 1 cup water
- 2 cups Parmesan cheese, for topping

Directions

1. First wash the zucchini and cut it lengthwise.
2. Take a skillet and heat oil in it.
3. Sauté the onion in olive oil for a few minutes.
4. Then add the quinoa and water and let it cook for 8 minutes with the lid on the top.
5. Transfer the quinoa to a bowl and add all remaining ingredients excluding zucchini and Parmesan cheese.
6. Scoop out the seeds of zucchinis.
7. Fill the cavity of zucchinis with bowl mixture.
8. Top it with a handful of Parmesan cheese.
9. Arrange 4 zucchinis in the air fryer basket.
10. Select the AIR FRY for 20 minutes and adjust the temperature to 390 degrees F.
11. Once done, serve and enjoy.

Serving Suggestion: Serve it with pasta.

Variation Tip: None.

Nutritional Information Per Serving: Calories 1171| Fat 48.6g| Sodium 1747mg | Carbs 132.4g | Fiber 42.1g | Sugar 11.5g | Protein 65.7g

Mixed Air Fry Veggies

Prep time: 15 minutes| **Cook time:** 25 minutes| **Serves:** 4

Ingredients

- 2 cups carrots, cubed
- 2 cups potatoes, cubed
- 2 cups shallots, cubed
- 2 cups zucchini, diced
- 2 cups yellow squash, cubed
- Salt and black pepper, to taste
- 1 tablespoon Italian seasoning
- 2 tablespoons ranch seasoning
- 4 tablespoons olive oil

Directions

1. Take a large bowl and add all the veggies to it.
2. Season the veggies with salt, pepper, Italian seasoning, ranch seasoning, and olive oil.
3. Toss all the ingredients well.
4. Now put it to the basket of the air fryer.
5. Set the unit to AIR FRY mode at 360 degrees F for 25 minutes.
6. Once it is cooked and done, serve, and enjoy.

Serving Suggestion: Serve it with rice.

Variation Tip: None.

Nutritional Information Per Serving:
Calories 275| Fat 15.3g| Sodium 129mg | Carbs 33g | Fiber 3.8g | Sugar 5g | Protein 4.4g

Air Fried Okra

Prep time: 10 minutes| **Cook time:** 13 minutes| **Serves:** 2

Ingredients:

- ½ lb. okra pods sliced
- 1 teaspoon olive oil
- ¼ teaspoon salt
- ⅛ teaspoon black pepper

Preparation:

1. At 375 degrees F, preheat your Air Fryer on Air Fry mode.
2. Toss okra with olive oil, salt, and black pepper in a bowl.
3. Spread the okra in a single layer in the Air Fryer Basket.
4. Return the Air Fryer Basket to the Air Fryer and cook for 13 minutes.
5. Initiate cooking by pressing the START/PAUSE BUTTON.
6. Toss the okra once cooked halfway through, and resume cooking.
7. Serve warm.

Serving Suggestion: Serve with potato chips and bread slices.

Variation Tip: Sprinkle cornmeal before cooking for added crispiness.

Nutritional Information Per Serving:
Calories 208 | Fat 5g |Sodium 1205mg | Carbs 34.1g | Fiber 7.8g | Sugar 2.5g | Protein 5.9g

Fresh Mix Veggies in Air Fryer

Prep time: 15 minutes| **Cook time:** 12 minutes| **Serves:** 4

Ingredients

- 1 cup cauliflower florets
- 1 cup carrots, peeled chopped
- 1 cup broccoli florets
- 2 tablespoons avocado oil
- Salt, to taste
- ½ teaspoon chili powder
- ½ teaspoon garlic powder
- ½ teaspoon herbs de Provence
- 1 cup parmesan cheese

Directions

1. Take a bowl, and add all the veggies to it.
2. Toss and then season the veggies with salt, chili powder, garlic powder, and herbs de Provence.
3. Toss it all well and then drizzle avocado oil.
4. Make sure the ingredients are coated well.
5. Now transfer the veggies to the basket of the air fryer.
6. Turn on the start button and set it to AIR FRY mode at 390 degrees for 10-12 minutes.
7. After 8 minutes of cooking, select the pause button and then take out the basket and sprinkle Parmesan cheese on top of the veggies.
8. Then let the cooking cycle complete for the next 3-4 minutes.
9. Once done, serve.

Serving Suggestion: Serve it with rice.

Variation Tip: Use canola oil or butter instead of avocado oil.

Nutritional Information Per Serving:

Calories161 | Fat 9.3g| Sodium 434mg | Carbs 7.7g | Fiber 2.4g | Sugar 2.5g | Protein 13.9

Kale and Spinach Chips

Prep time: 12 minutes| **Cook time:** 8 minutes| **Serves:** 2

Ingredients

- 2 cups spinach, torn in pieces and stem removed
- 2 cups kale, torn in pieces, stems removed
- 1 tablespoon olive oil
- Sea salt, to taste
- ⅓ cup Parmesan cheese

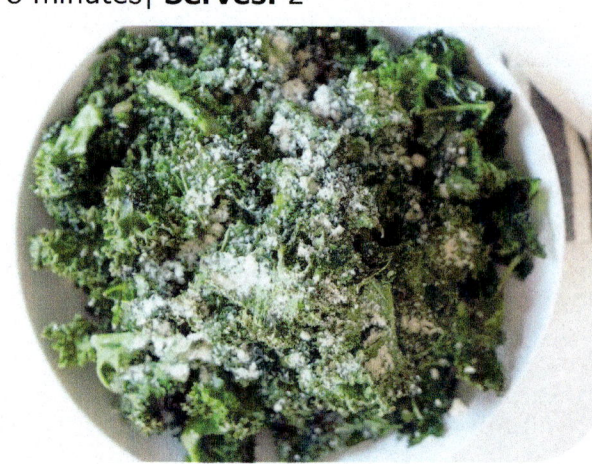

Directions

1. Take a bowl and add spinach to it.
2. Take another bowl and add kale to it.
3. Now, season both of them with olive oil, and sea salt.
4. Add kale and spinach to the basket of air fryer.
5. Select the AIR FRY mode at 350 degrees F for 8 minutes.
6. Once done, take out the crispy chips and sprinkle Parmesan cheese on top.
7. Serve and Enjoy.

Serving Suggestion: Serve it with baked potato.

Variation Tip: Use canola oil instead of olive oil.

Nutritional Information Per Serving:

Calories 166| Fat 11.1g| Sodium 355mg | Carbs 8.1g | Fiber 1.7g | Sugar 0.1g | Protein 8.2g

Brussels Sprouts

Prep time: 15 minutes| **Cook time:** 20 minutes| **Serves:** 2

Ingredients

- 2 pounds Brussels sprouts
- 2 tablespoons avocado oil
- Salt and pepper, to taste
- 1 cup pine nuts, roasted

Directions

1. Trim the bottom of Brussels sprouts.
2. Take a bowl and combine the avocado oil, salt, and black pepper.
3. Toss the Brussels sprouts well.
4. Transfer it to the air fryer basket.
5. Use AIR FRY mode for 20 minutes at 390 degrees F.
6. Once the Brussels sprouts get crisp and tender, take out and serve.

Serving Suggestion: Serve with rice.

Variation Tip: Use olive oil instead of avocado oil.

Nutritional Information Per Serving: Calories 672| Fat 50g| Sodium 115mg | Carbs 51g | Fiber 20.2g | Sugar 12.3g | Protein 25g

Desserts Recipes

Apple Hand Pies

Prep time: 15 minutes | **Cook time:** 21 minutes | **Serves:** 8

Ingredients:

- 8 tablespoons butter, softened
- 12 tablespoons brown sugar
- 2 teaspoons cinnamon, ground
- 4 medium Granny Smith apples, diced
- 2 teaspoons cornstarch
- 4 teaspoons cold water
- 1 (14 oz) package pastry, 9-inch crust pie
- Cooking spray
- 1 tablespoon grapeseed oil
- ½ cup powdered sugar
- 2 teaspoons milk

Preparation:

1. At 390 degrees F, preheat your Air Fryer on Air Fry mode.
2. Toss apples with brown sugar, butter, and cinnamon in a suitable skillet.
3. Place the skillet over medium heat and stir cook for 5 minutes.
4. Mix cornstarch with cold water in a small bowl.
5. Add cornstarch mixture into the apple and cook for 1 minute until it thickens.
6. Remove this filling from the heat and allow it to cool.
7. Unroll the pie crust and spray on a floured surface.
8. Cut the dough into 16 equal rectangles.
9. Wet the edges of the 8 rectangles with water and divide the apple filling at the center of these rectangles.
10. Place the other 8 rectangles on top and crimp the edges with a fork, then make 2-3 slashes on top.
11. Place the small pies in the Air Fryer Basket.
12. Return the Air Fryer Basket to the Air Fryer and cook for 17 minutes.
13. Initiate cooking by pressing the START/PAUSE BUTTON.
14. Flip the pies once cooked halfway through, and resume cooking.
15. Meanwhile, mix sugar with milk.
16. Pour this mixture over the apple pies.
17. Serve fresh.

Serving Suggestion: Serve with apple sauce.

Variation Tip: Add shredded nuts and coconuts to the filling.

Nutritional Information Per Serving:
Calories 284 | Fat 16g | Sodium 252mg | Carbs 31.6g | Fiber 0.9g | Sugar 6.6g | Protein 3.7g

Air Fried Beignets

Prep time: 15 minutes | **Cook time:** 21 minutes | **Serves:** 6

Ingredients:

- Cooking spray
- ¼ cup white sugar
- ⅛ cup water
- ½ cup all-purpose flour
- 1 large egg, separated
- 1 ½ teaspoons butter, melted
- ½ teaspoon baking powder
- ½ teaspoon vanilla extract
- 1 pinch salt
- 2 tablespoons confectioners' sugar, or to taste

Preparation:

1. At 390 degrees F, preheat your Air Fryer on Air Fry mode.
2. Beat flour with water, sugar, egg yolk, baking powder, butter, vanilla extract, and salt in a large bowl until lumps-free.
3. Beat egg whites in a separate bowl and beat using an electric hand mixer until it forms soft peaks.
4. Add the egg white to the flour batter and mix gently until fully incorporated.
5. Divide the dough into small beignets and place them in the Air Fryer Basket.
6. Return the Air Fryer Basket to the Air Fryer and cook for 17 minutes.
7. Initiate cooking by pressing the START/PAUSE BUTTON.
8. And cook for another 4 minutes. Dust the cooked beignets with sugar.
9. Serve.

Serving Suggestion: Serve with a dollop of sweet cream dip.

Variation Tip: Add chopped raisins and nuts to the dough.

Nutritional Information Per Serving:

Calories 327 | Fat 14.2g | Sodium 672mg | Carbs 47.2g | Fiber 1.7g | Sugar 24.8g | Protein 4.4g

Oreo Rolls

Prep time: 10 minutes| **Cook time:** 12 minutes| **Serves:** 9

Ingredients:

- 1 crescent sheet roll
- 9 Oreo cookies
- Cinnamon powder, to serve
- Powdered sugar, to serve

Preparation:

1. At 360 degrees F, preheat your Air Fryer on Air Fry mode.
2. Spread the crescent sheet roll and cut it into 9 equal squares.
3. Place one cookie at the center of each square.
4. Wrap each square around the cookies and press the ends to seal.
5. Place half of the wrapped cookies in the Air Fryer Basket.
6. Return the Air Fryer Basket to the Air Fryer and cook for 6 minutes.
7. Initiate cooking by pressing the START/PAUSE BUTTON.
8. Cook the remaining cookie rolls in the same way.
9. Garnish the rolls with sugar and cinnamon.
10. Serve.

Serving Suggestion: Serve a cup of spice latte or hot chocolate.

Variation Tip: Dip the rolls in melted chocolate for a change of taste.

Nutritional Information Per Serving:

Calories 175 | Fat 13.1g |Sodium 154mg | Carbs 14g | Fiber 0.8g | Sugar 8.9g | Protein 0.7g

Zesty Cranberry Scones

Prep time: 10 minutes| **Cook time:** 16 minutes| **Serves:** 8

Ingredients:

- 4 cups of flour
- ½ cup brown sugar
- 2 tablespoons baking powder
- ½ teaspoon ground nutmeg
- ½ teaspoon salt
- ½ cup butter, chilled and diced
- 2 cups fresh cranberry
- ⅔ cup sugar
- 2 tablespoons orange zest
- 1 ¼ cups half and half cream
- 2 eggs

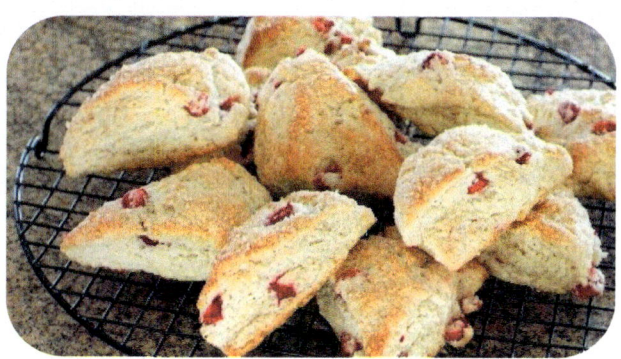

Preparation:

1. At 375 degrees F, preheat your Air Fryer on Air Fry mode.
2. Whisk flour with baking powder, salt, nutmeg, and both the sugars in a bowl.
3. Stir in egg and cream, mix well to form a smooth dough.
4. Fold in cranberries along with the orange zest.
5. Knead this dough well on a work surface.
6. Cut 3-inch circles out of the dough.
7. Place the scones in the Air Fryer Basket and spray them with cooking oil.
8. Return the Air Fryer Basket to the Air Fryer and cook for 16 minutes.
9. Initiate cooking by pressing the START/PAUSE BUTTON.
10. Flip the scones once cooked halfway and resume cooking.
11. Enjoy.

Serving Suggestion: Serve with cranberry jam on the side.

Variation Tip: Add raisins instead of cranberries to the dough.

Nutritional Information Per Serving:

Calories 204 | Fat 9g |Sodium 91mg | Carbs 27g | Fiber 2.4g | Sugar 15g | Protein 1.3g

Walnuts Fritters

Prep time: 15 minutes| **Cook time:** 15 minutes| **Serves:** 6

Ingredients:

- 1 cup all-purpose flour
- ½ cup walnuts, chopped
- ¼ cup white sugar
- ¼ cup milk
- 1 egg
- 1 ½ teaspoons baking powder
- 1 pinch salt
- Cooking spray
- 2 tablespoons white sugar
- ½ teaspoon ground cinnamon

Glaze:

- ½ cup confectioners' sugar
- 1 tablespoon milk
- ½ teaspoon caramel extract
- ¼ teaspoon ground cinnamon

Preparation:

1. At 375 degrees F, preheat your Air Fryer on Air Fry mode.
2. Layer the Air Fryer Basket with parchment paper.
3. Grease the parchment paper with cooking spray.
4. Whisk flour with milk, ¼ cup of sugar, egg, baking powder, and salt in a small bowl.
5. Separately mix 2 tablespoons of sugar with cinnamon in another bowl, toss in walnuts and mix well to coat.
6. Stir in flour mixture and mix until combined.
7. Drop the fritters mixture using a cookie scoop into the Air Fryer Basket.
8. Return the Air Fryer Basket to the Air Fryer and cook for 15 minutes.
9. Initiate cooking by pressing the START/PAUSE BUTTON.
10. Flip the fritters once cooked halfway through, then resume cooking.
11. Meanwhile, whisk milk, caramel extract, confectioners' sugar, and cinnamon in a bowl.
12. Transfer fritters to a wire rack and allow them to cool.
13. Drizzle with a glaze over the fritters.

Serving Suggestion: Serve with butter pecan ice cream or strawberry jam.

Variation Tip: Add maple syrup on top.

Nutritional Information Per Serving:

Calories 391 | Fat 24g |Sodium 142mg | Carbs 38.5g | Fiber 3.5g | Sugar 21g | Protein 6.6g

Biscuit Doughnuts

Prep time: 15 minutes| **Cook time:** 15 minutes| **Serves:** 8

Ingredients:

- ½ cup white sugar
- 1 teaspoon cinnamon
- ½ cup powdered sugar
- 1 can pre-made biscuit dough
- Coconut oil
- Melted butter to brush biscuits

Preparation:

1. At 375 degrees F, preheat your Air Fryer on Air Fry mode.
2. Place all the biscuits on a cutting board and cut holes in the center of each biscuit using a cookie cutter.
3. Grease the Air Fryer Basket with coconut oil.
4. Place the biscuits in the Air Fryer Basket while keeping them 1 inch apart.
5. Return the Air Fryer Basket to the Air Fryer and cook for 15 minutes.
6. Initiate cooking by pressing the START/PAUSE BUTTON.
7. Brush all the donuts with melted butter and sprinkle cinnamon and sugar on top.
8. Air fry these donuts for one minute more.
9. Enjoy.

Serving Suggestion: Serve the doughnuts with chocolate syrup on top.

Variation Tip: Inject strawberry jam into each doughnut.

Nutritional Information Per Serving:

Calories 192 | Fat 9.3g |Sodium 133mg | Carbs 27.1g | Fiber 1.4g | Sugar 19g | Protein 3.2g

Bread Pudding

Prep time: 12 minutes| **Cook time:** 8-12 minutes| **Serves:** 2

Ingredients

- Nonstick spray, for greasing ramekins
- 2 slices white bread, crumbled
- 4 tablespoons white sugar
- 5 large eggs
- ½ cup cream
- Salt, pinch
- ⅓ teaspoon cinnamon powder

Directions

1. Take a bowl and whisk eggs in it.
2. Add sugar and salt to the egg and whisk it all well.
3. Then add cream and use a hand beater to incorporate the entire ingredients.
4. Now add cinnamon, and add crumbs of bread.
5. Mix it well and add into a round shaped baking pan.
6. Put it inside the Ninja Air Fryer.
7. Set it on AIR FRY mode at 350 degrees F for 8-12 minutes.
8. Once it's cooked, serve.

Serving Suggestion: Serve it with Coffee.

Variation Tip: Use brown sugar instead of white sugar.

Nutritional Information Per Serving:

Calories 331| Fat16.1g| Sodium 331mg | Carbs 31g | Fiber0.2g | Sugar 26.2g | Protein 16.2g

Pumpkin Muffins

Prep time: 20 minutes| **Cook time:** 19 minutes| **Serves:** 4

Ingredients

- 1 and ½ cups all-purpose flour
- ½ teaspoon baking soda
- ½ teaspoon of baking powder
- 1 and ¼ teaspoons cinnamon, groaned
- ¼ teaspoon ground nutmeg, grated
- 2 large eggs
- Salt, pinch
- 3/4 cup granulated sugar
- ½ cup dark brown sugar
- 1 and ½ cups of pumpkin puree
- ¼ cup coconut milk

Directions

1. Take 4 ramekins that are the size of a cup and layer them with muffin papers.
2. Crack an egg in a bowl and add brown sugar, baking soda, baking powder, cinnamon, nutmeg, and sugar.
3. Whisk it all very well with an electric hand beater.
4. Now, in a second bowl, mix the flour, and salt.
5. Now, mix the dry ingredients slowly with the wet ingredients.
6. Now, at the end fold in the pumpkin puree and milk, mix it well
7. Divide this batter into 4 ramekins.
8. Now, put the ramekins inside the basket.
9. Add basket to the unit.
10. Set the time to 18 minutes at 360 degrees F at AIR FRY mode.
11. Check if not done, and let it AIR FRY for one more minute.
12. Once it is done, serve.

Serving Suggestion: Serve it with a glass of milk.

Variation Tip: Use almond milk instead of coconut milk.

Nutritional Information Per Serving:

Calories 291| Fat6.4 g| Sodium 241mg | Carbs 57.1g | Fiber 4.4g | Sugar42 g | Protein 5.9g

Lemony Sweet Twists

Prep time: 15 minutes| **Cook time:** 9 minutes| **Serves:** 2

Ingredients

- 1 box store-bought puff pastry
- ½ teaspoon lemon zest
- 1 tablespoon lemon juice
- 2 teaspoons brown sugar
- Salt, pinch
- 2 tablespoons Parmesan cheese, freshly grated

Directions

1. Put the puff pastry dough on a clean work area.
2. In a bowl, combine Parmesan cheese, brown sugar, salt, lemon zest, and lemon juice.
3. Press this mixture on both sides of the dough.
4. Now, cut the pastry into 1" x 4" strips.
5. Twist each of the strips.
6. Transfer it to the air fryer basket.
7. Select the air fry mode at 400 degrees F for 9-10 minutes.
8. Once cooked, serve and enjoy.

Serving Suggestion: Serve it with champagne!

Variation Tip: None.

Nutritional Information Per Serving:

Calories 156| Fat10g| Sodium 215mg | Carbs 14g | Fiber 0.4g | Sugar3.3 g | Protein 2.8g

Chocolate Chip Muffins

Prep time: 12 minutes| **Cook time:** 15 minutes| **Serves:** 2

Ingredients

- Salt, pinch
- 2 eggs
- ⅓ cup brown sugar
- ⅓ cup butter
- 4 tablespoons milk
- ¼ teaspoon vanilla extract
- ½ teaspoon baking powder
- 1 cup all-purpose flour
- 1 pouch chocolate chips, 35 grams

Directions

1. Take 4 oven-safe ramekins that are the size of a cup and layer them with muffin papers.
2. In a bowl, whisk the egg, brown sugar, butter, milk, and vanilla extract.
3. Whisk it all very well with an electric hand beater.
4. Now, in a second bowl, mix the flour, baking powder, and salt.
5. Now, mix the dry ingredients slowly into the wet ingredients.
6. Now, at the end fold in the chocolate chips and mix them well.
7. Divide this batter into 4 ramekins.
8. Now, put the ramekins in the basket.
9. Set the time to 15 minutes at 350 degrees F, on AIR FRY mode.
10. Check if not done, and let it AIR FRY for one more minute.
11. Once it is done, serve.

Serving Suggestion: Serve it with chocolate syrup drizzle.

Variation Tip: None.

Nutritional Information Per Serving:

Calories 757| Fat40.3g| Sodium 426mg | Carbs 85.4g | Fiber 2.2g | Sugar 30.4g | Protein 14.4g

Mini Blueberry Pies

Prep time: 12 minutes| **Cook time:** 10 minutes| **Serves:** 2

Ingredients

- 1 box store-bought pie dough, Trader Joe's
- ¼ cup blueberry jam
- 1 teaspoon lemon zest
- 1 egg white, for brushing

Directions

1. Take the store brought pie dough and cut it into 3-inch circles.
2. Brush the dough with egg white all around the parameters.
3. Now add blueberry jam and zest in the middle and top it with another circular.
4. Press the edges with the fork to seal it.
5. Make a slit in the middle of the dough and transfer it to the basket.
6. Set it to AIR FRY mode at 360 degrees for 10 minutes.
7. Once cooked, serve.

Serving Suggestion: Serve it with vanilla ice-cream.

Variation Tip: Use orange zest instead of lemon zest.

Nutritional Information Per Serving:
Calories 234| Fat 8.6g| Sodium 187mg | Carbs 38.2 g | Fiber 0.1g | Sugar13.7 g | Protein 2g

Air Fried Bananas

Prep time: 10 minutes| **Cook time:** 13 minutes| **Serves:** 4

Ingredients:

- 4 bananas, sliced
- 1 avocado oil cooking spray

Preparation:

1. At 350 degrees F, preheat your Air Fryer on Air Fry mode.
2. Spread the banana slices in the Air Fryer Basket in a single layer.
3. Drizzle avocado oil over the banana slices.
4. Return the Air Fryer Basket to the Air Fryer and cook for 13 minutes.
5. Initiate cooking by pressing the START/PAUSE BUTTON.
6. Serve.

Serving Suggestion: Serve with a dollop of vanilla ice-cream.

Variation Tip: Drizzle chopped nuts on top of the bananas.

Nutritional Information Per Serving:
Calories 149 | Fat 1.2g |Sodium 3mg | Carbs 37.6g | Fiber 5.8g | Sugar 29g | Protein 1.1g

Mini Strawberry and Cream Pies

Prep time: 12 minutes| **Cook time:** 10 minutes| **Serves:** 2

Ingredients

- 1 box Store-Bought Pie Dough, Trader Joe's
- 1 cup strawberries, cubed
- 3 tablespoons cream, heavy
- 2 tablespoons almonds
- 1 egg white, for brushing

Directions

1. Take the store brought pie dough and flatten it on a surface.
2. Use a round cutter to cut it into 3-inch circles.
3. Brush the dough with egg white all around the parameters.
4. Now add almonds, strawberries, and cream in a very little amount in the center of the dough, and top it with another circular.
5. Press the edges with the fork to seal it.
6. Make a slit in the middle of the dough and put it into the basket.
7. Set it to AIR FRY mode 360 degrees for 10 minutes.
8. Once done, serve.

Serving Suggestion: Serve it with vanilla ice-cream.

Variation Tip: Use orange zest instead of lemon zest.

Nutritional Information Per Serving:
Calories 203| Fat12.7g| Sodium 193mg | Carbs20 g | Fiber 2.2g | Sugar 5.8g | Protein 3.7g

4 Weeks Diet Plan

Week 1

Monday

Breakfast: Morning Patties

Lunch: Salmon Patties

Snack: Crispy Plantain Chips

Dinner: Beef Cheeseburgers

Dessert: Apple Hand Pies

Tuesday

Breakfast: Breakfast Sausage Omelet

Lunch: Salmon with Fennel Salad

Snack: Chicken Tenders

Dinner: Steak and Mashed Creamy Potatoes

Dessert: Mini Strawberry and Cream Pies

Wednesday

Breakfast: Egg with Baby Spinach

Lunch: Seafood Shrimp Omelet

Snack: Crispy Plantain Chips

Dinner: Parmesan Pork Chops

Dessert: Biscuit Doughnuts

Thursday

Breakfast: Crispy Hash Browns

Lunch: Two-Way Salmon

Snack: Sweet Bites

Dinner: Air Fried Turkey Breast

Dessert: Air Fried Bananas

Friday

Breakfast: Cinnamon Toasts

Lunch: Fried Artichoke Hearts

Snack: Salmon Nuggets

Dinner: Veggie Stuffed Chicken Breasts

Dessert: Zesty Cranberry Scones

Saturday

Breakfast: Pepper Egg Cups

Lunch: Salmon with Green Beans

Snack: Chili Chicken Wings

Dinner: Steak and Mashed Creamy Potatoes

Dessert: Bread Pudding

Sunday

Breakfast: Breakfast Bacon

Lunch: Kale and Spinach Chips

Snack: Brazilian Chicken Drumsticks

Dinner: Beef Ribs II

Dessert: Chocolate Chip Muffins

Week 2

Monday

Breakfast: Morning Patties

Lunch: Fresh Mix Veggies in Air Fryer

Snack: Chicken Crescent Wraps

Dinner: Mustard Rubbed Lamb Chops

Dessert: Chocolate Chip Muffins

Tuesday

Breakfast: Cinnamon Toasts

Lunch: Zucchini with Stuffing

Snack: Cheddar Quiche

Dinner: Steak in Air Fry

Dessert: Lemony Sweet Twists

Wednesday

Breakfast: Crispy Hash Browns

Lunch: Air Fried Okra

Snack: Blueberries Muffins

Dinner: Parmesan Pork Chops

Dessert: Apple Hand Pies

Thursday

Breakfast: Morning Patties

Lunch: Zucchini with Stuffing

Snack: Chicken Tenders

Dinner: Gochujang Brisket

Dessert: Chocolate Chip Muffins

Friday

Breakfast: Breakfast Bacon

Lunch: Fresh Mix Veggies in Air Fryer

Snack: Crispy Tortilla Chips

Dinner: Fried Lobster Tails

Dessert: Walnuts Fritters

Saturday

Breakfast: Crispy Hash Browns

Lunch: Green Beans with Baked Potatoes

Snack: Onion Rings

Dinner: Lemon Pepper Salmon with Asparagus

Dessert: Apple Hand Pies

Sunday

Breakfast: Pumpkin Muffins

Lunch: Mixed Air Fry Veggies

Snack: Blueberries Muffins

Dinner: Frozen Breaded Fish Fillet

Dessert: Air Fried Beignets

Week 3

Monday:

Breakfast: Morning Egg Rolls

Lunch: Fried Artichoke Hearts

Snack: Parmesan French Fries

Dinner: Scallops with Greens

Dessert: Air Fried Bananas

Tuesday

Breakfast: Banana and Raisins Muffins

Lunch: Green Beans with Baked Potatoes

Snack: Blueberries Muffins

Dinner: Cornish Hen with Asparagus

Dessert: Lemony Sweet Twists

Wednesday

Breakfast: Pumpkin Muffins

Lunch: Sweet Potatoes with Honey Butter

Snack: Chicken Tenders

Dinner: Chicken Breast Strips

Dessert: Air Fried Beignets

Thursday

Breakfast: Cinnamon Toasts

Lunch: Air Fried Okra

Snack: Parmesan French Fries

Dinner: Veggie Stuffed Chicken Breasts

Dessert: Bread Pudding

Friday

Breakfast: Crispy Hash Browns

Lunch: Quinoa Patties

Snack: Chicken Wings

Dinner: Yummy Chicken Breasts

Dessert: Oreo Rolls

Saturday

Breakfast: Banana and Raisins Muffins

Lunch: Brussels Sprouts

Snack: Sweet Bites

Dinner: Ham Burger Patties

Dessert: Lemony Sweet Twists

Sunday

Breakfast: Morning Egg Rolls

Lunch: Green Beans with Baked Potatoes

Snack: Parmesan French Fries

Dinner: Parmesan Pork Chops

Dessert: Air Fried Bananas

Week 4

Monday

Breakfast: Morning Patties

Lunch: Mixed Air Fry Veggies

Snack: Grill Cheese Sandwich

Dinner: Lamb Shank with Mushroom Sauce

Dessert: Bread Pudding

Tuesday

Breakfast: Pumpkin Muffins

Lunch: Fried Artichoke Hearts

Snack: Crispy Tortilla Chips

Dinner: Beef Ribs I

Dessert: Walnuts Fritters

Wednesday

Breakfast: Breakfast Bacon

Lunch: Kale and Spinach Chips

Snack: Crispy Plantain Chips

Dinner: Short Ribs & Root Vegetables

Dessert: Zesty Cranberry Scones

Thursday

Breakfast: Banana and Raisins Muffins

Lunch: Curly Fries

Snack: Chili Chicken Wings

Dinner: Gochujang Brisket

Dessert: Biscuit Doughnuts

Friday

Breakfast: Morning Patties

Lunch: Garlic Potato Wedges in Air Fryer

Snack: Blueberries Muffins

Dinner: Short Ribs & Root Vegetables

Dessert: Air Fried Bananas

Saturday

Breakfast: Egg with Baby Spinach

Lunch: Kale and Spinach Chips

Snack: Chicken Tenders

Dinner: Lamb Shank with Mushroom Sauce

Dessert: Biscuit Doughnuts

Sunday

Breakfast: Crispy Hash Browns

Lunch: Lemon Pepper Salmon with Asparagus

Snack: Crispy Plantain Chips

Dinner: Chinese BBQ Pork

Dessert: Mini Strawberry and Cream Pies

Conclusion

Whether you're finding an easy way to make French fries, make oven-baked chicken wings, or cook French toast sticks at breakfast without deep-frying—this air fryer will get you covered. The temperature setting ranging from 105°F to 400°F lets you quickly reheat and evenly cook your meals. With its compact and sleek design, it does not take up all your counter space. The one-touch control panel offers you greater functionality than an average air fryer. Ninja Foodi Air Fryer is the cooking partner you've always longed for, and It's a great addition to anyone's kitchen.

… Copyright 2021 - All rights reserved

This document is geared towards providing exact and reliable information with regards to the topic and issue covered. The publication is sold with the idea that the publisher is not required to render accounting, officially permitted, or otherwise, qualified services. If advice is necessary, legal, or professional, a practiced individual in the profession should be ordered. - From a Declaration of Principles which was accepted and approved equally by a Committee of the American Bar Association and a Committee of Publishers and Associations. In no way is it legal to reproduce, duplicate, or transmit any part of this document in either electronic means or in printed format. Recording of this publication is strictly prohibited and any storage of this document is not allowed unless with written permission from the publisher.

All rights reserved. The information provided herein is stated to be truthful and consistent, in that any liability, in terms of inattention or otherwise, by any usage or abuse of any policies, processes, or directions contained within is the solitary and utter responsibility of the recipient reader.

Under no circumstances will any legal responsibility or blame be held against the publisher for any reparation, damages, or monetary loss due to the information herein, either directly or indirectly. Respective authors own all copyrights not held by the publisher.

The information herein is offered for informational purposes solely, and is universal as

so. The presentation of the information is without contract or any type of guarantee assurance. The trademarks that are used are without any consent, and the publication of the trademark is without permission or backing by the trademark owner.

All trademarks and brands within this book are for clarifying purposes only and are the owned by the owners themselves, not affiliated with this document.

Printed in Great Britain
by Amazon